WE COME FIRST!

"This is the most important book written this century"

Albert Werden

WE COME FIRST!

ISBN: 1494738686
ISBN 13: 9781494738686
Library of Congress Control Number: 2014902070
CreateSpace Independent Publishing Platform
North Charleston, South Carolina

PART I

Opening

Big business, the US government, the mayors of cities, and the governors of states pushed for NAFTA and free-trade agreements to accommodate the greedy rich un-American international business executives that send American manufacturing jobs to third world countries. The employees of third world countries are paid between $.50 and $2.50 an hour which amounts to "slave labor". This practice of sending jobs out of the United States to maximize profits has robbed many Americans of their middle-class way of life. Some US companies that outsource jobs have claimed they are contributing to a global economy, but the bigger issue is that they're doing incredible damage to the US economy. And, as we will see, the American press has been complicit with business in this practice.

Sadness, despair, and poverty strikes many middle-class families in the United States because of the bias press along with the international executives of big business, that supports the outsourcing of American jobs that creates a nonexistent "fair global economy". Being employed at a job that gives a person the opportunity to achieve a dignified middle-class lifestyle is not the goal of the greedy, uncaring business executives. My definition of greed is accumulating wealth at any means. The end justifies the means. Using lies, bribery, intimidation, and other unethical means are perfectly acceptable to the greedy in their quest to accumulate wealth. Greed by definition is not admirable. Greed has led to the outsourcing of US manufacturing jobs, which has deprived many

Americans of the expectation that they can buy a car, own a home, take a vacation, and send their children off to college.

The employees that lost their jobs to slave labor countries paid state taxes, city taxes, County taxes, income taxes, sales taxes, and they paid into Social Security so money would be available during their retirement years. Do any of these slaves that make between $.50 to $2.50 an hour, pay US state taxes, US County taxes, US city taxes, US income taxes, US sales tax, or Social Security taxes to our government ? I guess not.

But despite the situation described above the biased American press is happy to trot out a collection of experts who claim that outsourcing jobs to slave labor countries is the best thing that's happened to the United States since sliced bread. How these reporters and news commentators sleep at night, knowing that they support the destruction of millions of middle-class families is beyond me. Of course since they're paid well, they will say anything to keep their jobs.

We come first!

Our country is slowly being destroyed by their words and their loyalty to the rich. The press claims to be the eyes and ears of all citizens of the United States. In their twisting of the truth that favors the rich they've forfeited the right to that prestigious honor. With their half truths and twisting of the truth they've missed their mark.

The destruction of the middle-class has been taking place over the past twenty years since the passage of NAFTA and free-trade agreements **(unfair trade agreements)**, the effects of which have been further aggravated by the lack of effective tariffs. Manufacturing companies dislike dealing with US regulatory agencies and are always looking for some excuse to move their businesses to cheaper and less restrictive countries with no EPA, no OSHA, no unions, no lawyers, or any other impediments to their greed. Our government used NAFTA and a free trade philosophy to open up the labor market to the third world for business at the request of un-American US corporate executives. This was accomplished with the help of our biased national news outlets who brainwashed our middle-class citizens into thinking an unfair global economy was good for our US manufacturing workers.

Also contributing to the problem was a lack of resistance by the unions (AFL CIO, Teamsters, UAW, teachers union and others), along with AARP(American Association for Retired People), and the other organizations that expressed concern for the middle-class has caused the downfall of the American manufacturing workers. All this is being accomplished in the name of global economy. Another meaning for global economy is the sucking of American manufacturing jobs out of the United States of America along with the destruction of the base wage of American manufacturing workers. Base wages are what manufacturing employees were paid for each individual skill approximately seven years ago. An example, mold setters received approximately $15-$25 an hour around 2007, in the year 2013 a mold setter's pay can be as small as minimum wage. This huge loss of earning power by the middle-class employees was created by NAFTA, unfair trade agreements, and the lack of effective tariffs. NAFTA and unfair trade agreements were supported by the un-American international business community and the un-American news media that favors the rich. The greedy rich in this country, the so-called pillars of American businesses are laughing and ridiculing the brainwashed middle-class citizens

Telling half truths and twisting the truth is what the national news organizations do best. The press thinks middle-class citizens are stupid and easily swayed. To believe the global economy is good for the American worker, would require a lobotomy.

How you can tell if you have been lobotomized? If you believe that sending American jobs that paid between $15-$30 an hour to low wage countries that now pay as little as $.50 to $2.50 an hour for the same job and this is good for the US economy you've been lobotomized.

The creation of NAFTA was endorsed by large un-American international businesses that eventually became the biggest contributors to the financial destruction of millions of middle-class American families. In the beginning NAFTA was promoted as an agent in curbing illegal immigrants from crossing the border from Mexico to the United States. People from Europe, the Far East, people everywhere including Mexico want to live in a safe environment while reaching for the brass ring of prosperity. In Mexico drug lords ride roughshod over the population and perpetuate mass killings creating an unstable environment that has left many innocent bystanders lying dead in the streets. The Mexican people also know that making slave labor wages in a lawless society does not open the doors to a middle-class lifestyle. NAFTA never stopped or slowed down the illegal crossing of our borders by the Mexican people.

NAFTA was also expected to raise the lifestyle of the Mexican workers so they could become consumers of American products. After 20 years of big business lying and robbing the American manufacturing worker of their livelihood, the pay scale in Mexico now hovers around $.50 to $2.50 an hour which amounts to, slave labor.

Every day you can see the benefits of the global economy at work. Unemployment in the United States at 7% percent along with the underemployed, part-time employee and the forgotten citizens, those numbers could easily reach as high as 25 million American workers looking for a job with dignity and fair pay. With that many people in poverty a new third world country could easily be taking shape.

Approaching old age I have seen good times along with recessions. In the past, recovery from the recessions seemed to rebound in a reasonable amount of time. During the Reagan administration unemployment reached as high as 11% percent, so high unemployment and hard times are not new in this country. At that time we were still using the tariff system to create a level playing field for middle-class manufacturing workers. Not only did we recover from that recession and the unacceptable unemployment rate but we woke up to a booming economy.

Just imagine where the United States would be today if unfair trade agreements and the outsourcing of American manufacturing jobs to third world countries had happened during the Reagan administration. The United States recovery from that recession would have never taken place. That means unemployment remaining high along with the erosion of the wage base of American workers. Does that ring a bell? President Reagan understood the United States needs a balanced workforce of manufacturing jobs and high-tech jobs if we are to maintain the stability of the middle-class.

President Reagan also understood that a healthy economy requires effective tariffs to level the playing field for the middle-class manufacturing worker.

Our free-trade agreements with Mexico and other countries must be repealed along with the other free-trade agreements. Doing this and reestablishing effective tariffs could put a spark back in the US economy returning the United States back to full employment. Competing against workers making noncompetitive wages is not realistic but many of the multinational business people call this a global economy. Maintaining free trade status with Mexico is never going to help the United States reestablish a balanced work force. An excuse that big business makes is that they can't compete in a global market without moving American manufacturing jobs in slave labor countries such as Mexico.

Americans do not have a problem with American companies opening up businesses in Third World countries, as long as they sell their products to Third World countries. But this is a joke. They have little opportunity to sell to manufacturing workers in third world countries because big business doesn't pay their foreign employees enough money to become consumers. Our concerns arise when these products land on our shores, tariff free. When this happens the destruction of middle-class wage base along with the loss of millions and millions of middle-class manufacturing jobs takes place. Big business's main goal is manufacturing products with cheap foreign slave labor, creating an opportunity to sell their products in high labor markets.

Just look at Bangladesh and the collapse of a poorly constructed building that housed over a 1000 garment workers. Approximately 700 Bangladesh slaves perished in this unnecessary tragedy. Most of the employees in the garment industries have families which include husbands, wives, and children. The loss of a family member in Bangladesh is just as traumatic to the families as a life lost in the United States. Articles appeared in business magazines trying to put a positive spin on this tragic event. The authors of these articles claim $2 a day are good wages in Bangladesh and the garment workers should be happy because they are working toward becoming prosperous consumers. How does one become a consumer with a wage of $38 a month? Many greedy business executives have spent 50 years of exploiting the poor by creating an atmosphere that tolerates inhumane working conditions. Two dollars a day are good wages in the year 2013? A major sickness of right and wrong has taken over the un-American international business community. If outsourcing American jobs and the unnecessary printing of money doesn't stop now we might become one of those third world countries.

How rich African-Americans can support businesses that use slave labor in foreign countries is troubling. They (African-Americans) constantly complain about the mistreatment and abuse that African-Americans slaves endured from southern plantation owners for hundreds of years. The plantation owners in the South justified using slaves by saying that, without slaves they would not be able to harvest their crops at a reasonable cost. They also argued that a life of slavery in America was better than a life of squalor in Africa. Besides, how can the plantation owners become rich if slaves earned a living wage. Many rich African-Americans that own stock in companies that outsource African-American jobs to Third World countries gives the impression that they support slave labor. Supporting the outsourcing of African-American jobs to third world countries establishes many rich African-Americans in the United States as the new plantation owners in foreign countries. Many rich African Americans support CEOs and board members of companies that send non-college-educated African-American jobs to slave labor countries. These type of rich African-Americans have little sympathy for their brothers and sisters and their children that remain in poverty and live in areas riddled with crime and violence as long as they get richer.

Brainwashing!

Beware TV viewers you are about to be brainwashed by the national news organizations with the help and guidance of big business but if you're not in the mood to be brainwashed please change the channel now.

This disclaimer should precede every news show.

Brainwashing is one of the prime functions of news organizations. Continually saying the same thing over and over with the goal of convincing people of a particular viewpoint is called brainwashing. There are tricks news organization's use to sway public opinion. They specialize in statements like "a reliable source says," and "we referred to the experts". The majority of the experts that news organizations bring on their show are the same business people that are sending American jobs to slave labor countries or own stock in companies that support the outsourcing of American manufacturing jobs. Most of these so-called experts benefit financially from the outsourcing of middle-class manufacturing jobs. The news organizations are continually trying to convince people that the unfair global economy is a good thing for the United States. How the global economy is helping the middle-class is beyond me. If the unemployed manufacturing worker thinks that it's good for America to send seven jobs out of this country and receive one job in return then I guess the brainwashing is working.

PART I: BRAINWASHING!

We come first should be the motto of every middle-class person. The national mainstream news organizations report the unemployment figures along with how many people were able to obtain employment each month. But they don't tell you how many jobs were sent to slave labor countries like, Mexico, China, India, Bangladesh, Vietnam, and many other third world countries. Maybe they feel sending jobs out of this country doesn't affect employment. It's inexcusable for CNN, ABC, CBS, and NBC to refrain from reporting the number of manufacturing jobs being sent to third world countries. Constantly telling half the story and twisting the truth is what mainstream news organizations do best. This is **brainwashing** at its best. Always remember that many of these news organizations are controlled by greedy un-American corporate executives, who don't give one good shit about middle-class workers or this country. Their main goal is to enrich themselves by any means possible. Words like honesty and honor are not part of their vocabulary. It looks today as if the destruction of the middle-class's lifestyle is their main goal.

We come first!

CNN and the national news organizations **(American job destroyers)** talk about the fact that the US debt is increasing each minute, each hour, each day, and each year, but the reason why seems to have eluded the unethical press. Since September 30, 2012 the national debt is increasing at a rate of $2.7 billion each day. That means each citizen in the United States owes the government approximately $54,000. There's only one reason why this is happening and that is the outsourcing of American manufacturing jobs to slave labor countries. I guess CNN and the news organizations feel lowering the national debt without non college educated middle-class citizens having jobs is attainable. Most business executives thinks lowering our national debt is an easy task, just slash Social Security, Medicare, assisted housing, unemployment benefits, Medicaid, assistance to education, and other middle-class benefits because the greedy rich don't rely on these entitlements. Cut workers salaries, slash pensions, and eliminate jobs, all this so the rich can get richer. Now you know why our country is on the ropes and slipping fast. **Repealing NAFTA and unfair trade agreements while creating effective tariffs is the only way our country can return to the glory days of old. There is absolutely no other way.**

There is always a reason why news organizations omit part of a story and most of the time it is self- serving. The mainstream national news organizations needs revenue to continue operating, that translates into "we don't piss off our advertisers." When our national news organizations fail to report honestly on the economy it is taking its toll on our country. Middle-class workers are confused. Brainwashing by the national news organizations has led the middle-class into believing an unfair global economy is beneficial for American workers. Competing against foreign labor is destroying the American workforce.

CNN and the mainstream news organizations can find their way into Syria to film and report on the civil war each day. The national news organizations found their way into Libya to bring their viewers a first-hand account of the downfall of Gaddafi. Egypt is also a country in turmoil that receives attention from US news organizations. But gaining entrance into Mexico must be an impossible task, because the filming and reporting on the construction sites in Mexico is nonexistent. The completed construction sites and the new ones in progress are for only one reason, to steal American manufacturing jobs. Showing these sites will give middle-class manufacturing workers a glimpse into their future, unemployment and becoming part of the 47% percent receiving government assistance. If you believe sending jobs to Mexico and other slave labor countries is beneficial to the United States and its manufacturing workers it's only because you have been subjected to unethical news reporting by the biased press.

The unethical journalism taking place in the newsrooms of our local and national TV and radio stations adds to the heartbreak of our unemployed and underemployed manufacturing workers. The local and national news organizations whether they are TV or radio, are doing an injustice to their listeners and viewers. Not exposing NAFTA and the unfair trade agreements as the most un-American and anti-productive agreements since the beginning of time is unconscionable. Does anyone on the local level feel the manufacturing worker is getting a fair deal? The majority of American citizens feel outsourcing American manufacturing jobs is contributing to the rise in our national debt. They also feel outsourcing is the main cause of high unemployment and underemployed citizens of the United States. Each citizen has an obligation to speak out against NAFTA and unfair trade agreements. Contacting your local radio talk shows to express your feelings about these agreements can help. Encourage your local radio talk show to support their listeners by saying before and after each and every show. **"We support the repeal of NAFTA and the unfair trade agreements."** Our country needs some grassroots opposition to the collapse of our manufacturing workforce. The United States is never going to recover and be a great country again unless these agreements are abolished. A grass roots opposition to NAFTA could turn into a national referendum condemning the outsourcing of American jobs.

Many CEOs and board members of companies make fun of brainwashed middle-class citizens. After the giggles are over they meet with some of the mainstream national news organizations and complain that the middle-class entitlements such as Social Security, Medicare, subsidize housing, unemployment and other entitlements are bankrupting this country. The following day many news organizations explaining to their viewers, listeners, and readers that their experts feel middle-class entitlements are bringing America to its knees. US jobs being moved to slave labor countries by the millions will not even be discussed. Brainwashing by the news media never stops.

Global economy stands for the sucking of US jobs out of the United States to third world countries because there isn't any US income tax, no OSHA, no EPA, no lawyers, no Social Security tax, no state tax, no city tax, no sales tax, and discrimination against older workers and women is acceptable. With the aid of slave labor, these multinational companies put American workers at a major disadvantage. The products produced by these companies are imported back into the United States which has destroyed the manufacturing wage base of US workers. These rich leeches have destroyed the middle-class wage base to the tune of $7 to $13 an hour. Press operators a few years ago earned $15 to $30 an hour. With high unemployment you have too many people chasing too few jobs, this puts the employee at a major disadvantage and the employer in the driver seat and that's why press operators are now paid $8 to $9 an hour. The employer can now offer employment at a much lower wage. If people need jobs they have no choice but to accept the job at reduced pay. Your chances of hearing the truth from CNN and other news organizations are slim to none. The destruction of the middle-class manufacturing workers wage base, has cost middle-class manufacturing workers between $5000 and $20,000 a year. We need the middle-class workers to speak out against the greedy rich un-American CEOs that send US jobs to slave labor countries and the news manipulators who are complicit with them. In this way, we can restore the middle-class to its rightful place. Speaking out against un-American big business without the support of well-known TV or movie personalities, major figures in business, or the support of CNN and the national news organizations is a difficult task for the average middle-class manufacturing worker. Always remember this: **we come first** not Mexico, not China, not India, but workers in the good old USA.

Some news organizations air TV specials that examine current news events. Some of the specials are about crimes that have gone unpunished and the cover-up that followed. Some TV news specials report on scams pulled on the unsuspecting public, such as Ponzi schemes. But reporting on the biggest scam since the beginning of time is nonexistent. The mainstream national news organizations are part of that cover-up. These news organizations claim to be the eyes and ears of the public, exposing the criminals and their crimes along with the everyday challenges of middle-class life. But to most people it seems the TV news media main goal is to trick middle class America into thinking the unfair global economy is for their benefit.

Some news organizations bring different experts on their stations to explain about our troubled economy to their viewers. Their experts seem to be stockbrokers, hedge fund employees, and rich people expressing their opinions concerning our economy. All these so-called experts invest in companies that have transferred American manufacturing jobs to slave labor countries. Each one of these so-called experts will explain to the brainwashed American public that the unfair global economy is doing great. Being part of the unfair global economy will create millions of new jobs for the people of the United States. These statements made by their experts **are** lies! The only way the US American manufacturing worker can compete in an unfair global economy is by drastically having their pay slashed to $2-$3 an hour with few benefits. The only other option is to use effective tariffs to create a level playing field for our manufacturing workers. There is absolutely no other way.

Each expert who offers an opinion on the economy for news shows should say whether he or she has a vested interest in businesses that outsource American jobs. Dialogue between anti-outsourcing experts and pro-outsourcing experts being discussed in an open forum on national TV stations is never going to take place.

There is absolutely no benefit to the American manufacturing worker supporting NAFTA or unfair trade agreements. NAFTA and the unfair trade agreements are the job destroyers of future generations.

We come first!

We need jobs, not lies, not promises, not distortions. We need jobs! The middle-class manufacturing worker does not want to be part of Mitt Romney's 47% percent.

On Friday May 3 2013 CNN was at it again the half-truths with misleading statements, trying to compromise the middle class's ability to make independent decisions. With the jobs report coming out, CNN was using their own brand of distortion. They reported that 165,000 jobs had been added to the payrolls of businesses. This is not acceptable. That number is close to the break even point that's needed each month. The United States needs to add at least 350,000 to 450,000 jobs each and every month to put a legitimate dent in long-term unemployment. Achieving that goal can only be accomplished by **repealing NAFTA and the unfair trade agreements and by putting legitimate tariffs on goods coming in to the United States. There is absolutely no other way.**

CNN's spin on job growth for the month of April:

Retail jobs 29,000

WE COME FIRST!

Professional and business services 73,000
Manufacturing 00000
Wholesale trade 29,000
Leisure and hospitality 43,000
Healthcare 19,000

Activity in each of the above areas was qualified and discussed. But one area was conspicuous by its absence: manufacturing. Is this because the news organizations are in bed with the un-American multinational business executives and their boards of directors? They're just as guilty of destroying the US economy and the middle-class's future, but they're doing it by brainwashing? With manufacturing at zero growth how was CNN going to put a positive spin on that segment of the jobs report?

We can only speculate on the statement that might have been made during the meeting at CNN before reporting on the economy. How are we going to report on manufacturing at zero growth and keep the stupid ass middle-class stupid? Oh yes we just won't talk about manufacturing. Not one time was outsourcing of American jobs discuss leaving the viewer with a distorted impression of the US economy. CNN and the news media have a difficult time giving an honest journalistic view of our cherished citizens future. Every time the economy is discussed presenting all the facts that effect employment must be discussed and that means the outsourcing of jobs to slave labor countries!

Manufacturing having zero growth indicates the direction this country is going and who is supporting the destruction of the middle-class. Through the years manufacturing jobs have always paid well and a college degree was not mandatory. What was important was having a high school diploma or equivalent. The people that worked at those jobs supported millions upon millions of other jobs because they bought:

(1) Homes: carpenters lost their jobs, pipefitters lost their jobs, electricians lost their jobs, carpet layers lost their jobs, brick layers lost their jobs, landscapers lost their jobs, architects have lost their jobs, the future apprentices for each one of these trades never materialized

(2) Cars: With full employment the United States should be selling at least 18 to 19 million cars per year. We would need to employ more press operators, die setters, car and truck sales people, mechanics, machinists, die makers.

(3) Furniture, appliances, boats, vacations, taking the family out to dinner, and much more

The manufacturing jobs and service jobs paid $15 to $30 an hour. Now they are lost to the slaves of third world countries.

Sanity must return to our shores.

Many middle-class families are suffering. Homes are being foreclosed, car repossessed, children are being denied the basic enjoyments of childhood, and parents are being denied a job because of the transferring of US manufacturing jobs supported by the un-American biased press.

Lately the press has been reminding their viewers of the millions of jobs that have been created over the past few years. The American people are receiving a distorted view of the employment picture in the United States. The millions of jobs that have been created over the past few years are just keeping the United States at a breakeven point. To maintain the 7% to 7 1/2% percent unemployment, between 165,000 to 200,000 jobs must be created each month. At this time at least 2 million new jobs a year are needed to maintain our current pace of employment. Those who place any credibility on an upward spiral of employment based on the millions of jobs that have been created over the past few years are just dreaming. The United States needs between 350,000 to 450,000 jobs added to the employment picture each month to have any sizable impact on the unemployment. This translates into a need for 4 to 5 million new jobs each year. Even at that rate it will take years to get back to full employment. Middle-class manufacturing worker who think the economy is going to turn around any time soon has probably been watching too much CNN.

The possibility that the TV news networks might do a special to inform the public about the biggest scam since the beginning of time is quite remote. People that are fortunate enough to be working in manu-facturing may feel that their jobs are secure, but they're wrong. Their jobs may be the next to go. Just look at General Motors and the progress it's made since the 2009 citizen bailout. Spending billions of dollars of taxpayers money saved hundreds of thousands of jobs. The billions of tax dollars spent for the good of the country. But what country are we talking about? Mexico is getting almost $1 billion of General Motors's money (US taxpayers money) for expansion of their truck production and a new transmission plant. In the United States General Motors plans to support the US economy by spending $ 200 million in upgrades. Not one time have I heard of the Mexican government spending one red cent toward the bailout of General Motors. United States citizens spends their hard earned money keeping General Motors out of bankruptcy and the thanks that the hard-working manufacturing worker gets is the one finger wave and Mexico seems to be getting all the jobs. General Motors isn't the only automotive company to expand in Mexico. All the auto-motive companies that sell cars in the United States are in the process of expanding in Mexico or are planning to do so in the near future. After the automotive companies cars and trucks are built, driving them across the border is the next step.

Someone or some group must step up and convince the national news networks that their current way of reporting on the economy and on outsourcing of jobs is not acceptable. They are assisting big business in the destruction of the livelihood and future of a major part of working class America.

Supporting a tariff on incoming goods to the United States to create a level playing field for American manufacturing workers makes good sense. Using an effective tariff is a must because most

American manufacturing businesses struggle to compete in an unfair global economy, where slave wages are common in the foreign workforce. When the national news media reports on the economy and jobs, a clear and full view must be presented to the American people. Using the tariff system is not a new idea it's been around for a 100 years. We need jobs! The national news organizations along with business executives and their board members are promoting the destruction of the middle-class by their half truths and twisting of the truth.

In reporting, for example, John was killed does CNN and the other news outlets leave it that way or do they explain how he got killed? Did he die in a car accident, fall off a roof, crash his motorcycle, drowned, shot, did he have a heart attack, or did some other mishap occur? Without an explanation of how John died, you are left in limbo.

When CNN and other news outlets discuss our poor economy and high unemployment, outsourcing American manufacturing jobs is never discussed. They'll give you an in-depth reason why John died but the real reason why the United States has high unemployment and under-employment is not debate.

The unethical reporting that comes out of the newsrooms of our national press:

(1)   Has a negative impact on employment in the United States.

(2)   Has an unbalanced effect on the African-American community.

(3)   Has caused the devastation of future lives in the American manufacturing community.

(4)   Has cheated millions of children out of their childhoods because standing in line at food banks and soup kitchens are now their new play areas.

(5)   Has expose themselves to millions of viewers as uncaring with little regard for the average citizen and how greed has overtaken their executive offices.

(6)   And much more.

Our American news organizations unethical journalistic views on the US economy has cost the U.S. Treasury billions and billions of dollars. Distorting the truth must stop. Please give your viewers and listeners an honest assessment of the US economy. Eliminating your one-sided reporting may give hope to the unemployed and underemployed citizens of this great country.

When the national news organizations discuss the lack of revenue that each state is experiencing and the huge deficits our country is experiencing at this time, avoiding the truth and misleading the public are standard policy. If the un-American international business executives, with the support of the national news organizations did not have the opportunity to export millions upon millions of US manufacturing jobs to slave labor countries the United States would not be experiencing the economical climate that we are facing today. The millions and millions of Americans that had their jobs outsourced to third world countries would be buying homes, cars, paying state taxes, city tax, federal taxes, Social Security taxes, sales taxes, and much more. The crisis in home construction, states revenues, federal revenue, and much more would be over.

NAFTA and the unfair trade agreements must be abolished and effective tariffs established to stimulate our economy and regulate job losses and trade imbalances. There is no such thing as a global economy in which American manufacturing workers can compete. **Citizens, you must take your country back from the un-American biased press.**

Our country is slowly sinking into the sea of despair because our leaders have abandoned us. The sharks are having a field day with our future, they are eating us alive while the government and news networks overlook our cries for help. All middle-class manufacturing workers are asking for are jobs so they can save their children from poverty and crime that plagues their future.

Unregulated banks and subprime mortgages has caused a banking crisis in this country that has created a downturn in our economy and it may take decades to recover. These were the news headlines by the national news media at one time. In the beginning this was thought to be true, but the banking crisis has long passed and now we have the **"job"** crisis that is destroying the middle-class manufacturing worker's lifestyle. When big business looks into our future and says it may take decades for our economy to recover. The national press reports this to the brainwashed middle-class as breaking news. Such reporting reduces grumbling from the middle-class and makes it easier for the rich un-American international business executives to outsource American manufacturing jobs. If a group complains that jobs being sent to slave labor countries causes unemployment to remain high, the chances of this being reported on the network news is slim to none.

Our country is in deep peril and expecting big business to come to our rescue is futile, because it's never going to happen. One self-centered egotistical multibillionaire businessman echoed his thoughts by saying the United States has a **right to print money**. He is wrong, the United States does not have the right to print money. He is one of the international businesspeople who are destroying our country. Printing money as some un-American businesspeople have suggested is causing the stock market to manufacture another bubble. Buying stocks at this level is dangerous because once the federal government announces that printing money to keep the economy afloat will come to an end, the stock market will show its true colors. But the way things look the federal government and its employees have lost their minds, so printing money will continue until we've lost all credibility with the world. Of course the rich are laughing all the way to the bank.

If our treasury continues to support this runaway economy by printing money, the downfall of the United States economy will eventually take place. At one time Greece felt printing money was their right. In retrospect Greece would no doubt have second thoughts. Spending more than you take in is a sure sign of stupidity. Bankruptcy is inevitable. Our country is just as vulnerable as any other country. Stupidity can only last so long, the piper eventually needs to be paid.

Our country needs a press that supports the rich, poor, and middle-class. It also needs leaders with some common sense and a love for their country.

During the election of our congressional leaders many accusations and claims are made. The national news media creates a pedestal so their news commentators can stand above everyone else creating a god-like experience for their viewers. The press has appointed itself as the fact checkers. Where are the **fact checkers** when the press twists the truth about our economy? Where are the **fact checkers** when the press reports half the truth about our economy? The citizens of the United States need **fact checkers** to expose the truths about our national news networks.

Don Lemon

Don Lemon must be a semi blind, hearing impaired, very naïve news commentator on CNN during the weekends. When Don closes his eyes, he wonders why he can't see. He puts his hands over his ears and wonders why he can't hear. He stands in the middle of a forest and wonders why there are no trees. He and the African-American community are standing in quicksand and wonder why they can't see their knees. His goal is to change or alter the way a large portion of Americans views most of the African-American community. He should open up his eyes, removed his hands from his ears, step away from the forest, and keep his feet out of the quicksand. Then maybe just maybe he will understand that he is working for the most biased and racist news network in the world.

CNN represents itself as a balanced news network reporting for all nationalities and economic segments of this country. CNN's unfair reporting, showing favoritism toward the rich and powerful, is obvious to me. Maybe I'm the only one that sees CNN's one-sided reporting on the economy and their attempt to brainwash the masses. They continually use the phrase" global economy". In my opinion, in a true global economy all countries would be on a level playing field with regard to jobs and competition for projects that create jobs. How can the American manufacturing workers compete against slave labor countries when there is such a huge disparity between the wages paid in the United States and the wages paid in third world countries. The manufacturing jobs that the international business executives and their board of directors send to foreign countries pay between $.50 and $2.50 an hour. In the United States the same jobs used to pay between $15 and $30 an hour. I would like to know how the national news media can call this a level playing field for our American manufacturing workers. Global economy, in the vernacular of the media and big business stands for the destruction of the future of non-college-educated citizens of the United States. Somehow, the news media will turn their answer into a pretzel, confusing the middle-class and favoring their rich and powerful buddies. When the national news media reports on the economy and expresses concern about the lack of jobs, reporting on the millions and millions of jobs being sent to slave labor countries just in the past few years is nonexistent. Our country needs fact checkers to fact check CNN's biased news reporters. Don Lemon open up your eyes, clean out your ears, and get your feet out of the quicksand. Maybe you will understand my opinion of CNN and the national news organizations.

CNN's lack of honest reporting affects all people black, white, brown, red, yellow, and others. It affects the African-American communities disproportionately. Jobs are the only cure for African-Americans to eliminate poverty, crime, and violence in their communities. It has been said that education is the best method for the poor to become a middle-class citizens. But this has been tried and the percentage of citizens moving out of poverty by way of education is not acceptable. **We need jobs!**

We come first!

America needs a balanced economy, and that means college educated jobs along with non-college-educated jobs that pays a living wage.

At this time non college educated jobs that respects one's dignity and pays a living wage are challenging at best to find. Most state's manufacturing workforces have been slashed between 2.5 % and 4.5 % and at this time recovery still looks off in the far distant future, if at all. **This must change, starting immediately using effective tariffs is the only way to protect our domestic employees.** There are thousands of industries located in the United States that would like to continue operations in this country. The struggles of thousands of small manufacturing companies continue to multiply. Many in their work force have had their work week shortened, have been laid off, or have been forced to take pay cuts

Don Lemon remember, take your hands off your ears so you can hear what your own news organization says and what it doesn't say. CNN and the national news media claim small businesses are the backbone of this country, employing millions of people. Hearing an explanation as to why thousands and thousands of these business's doors have closed hasn't arrived yet. There is no secret why the entrepreneurs of these businesses are suffering. The employees of these American businesses cannot compete against slave labor. The American worker needs to believe in themselves again. The news media is misrepresenting the facts about their ability to compete in and unfair global market. Feelings of inadequacy has crept into their souls causing despair and doubts about their future. Many good hard-working Americans have given up hope of finding a job and have lost their way by dropping out of the mainstream of society, this has to change. Reporting honestly and fairly may renew hope for the future.

Don Lemon, the enthusiasm, dedication, and love that you have demonstrated for helping the African-American community is inspiring. Your voice came through loud and clear. They say an alcoholic first has to recognize that he or she is an alcoholic before changes can take place. The same goes for recognizing the problems in many African-American communities. Normally someone that criticizes the African-American communities is usually labeled a racist, even though helping the African-American community maybe their main goal.

I watched your commentary on the "N" word. The use of the "N" word is not the major problem in African-American households, or white households, or many other struggling households. Your voice should be heard on a commentary about the "J" word "jobs". The African-American community will never prosper or alter their way of life without jobs. The problem is most of the non-college-educated blacks and white's jobs have been sent to slave labor countries by the rich un-American international CEOs and their boards of directors who don't give one good shit about this country. Most international CEOs have preferred to live in the United States and enjoy all the freedoms we enjoy. The problem is that loving and caring for the United States is not a priority. The almighty dollar is their God. If NAFTA and the unfair trade agreements are not repealed and effective tariffs put in place, many African-American households, Hispanic households, and white households will never prosper or reach middle-class status. Since you live in a mainly African-American neighborhood, check around and see how many of your neighbors are willing to work for between $.50 and $2.50 an hour. Because this is the only way they can compete in this unfair global economy without an effective tariff.

Many times through the years CNN and the national news media **(job destroyers)** have had different businessmen as guest. They express their concerns about the direction the government is taking to create jobs. Their demeanor is so sad that you almost want to cry. They give the impression that their hearts goes out to the unemployed and under-employed. These businessmen also chastise the government for creating so much debt. They give their opinion on what the government should do to curb some of the debt. Usually their remedy falls on the shoulders of the middle-class citizens. They would, eliminating or reduce Social Security, Medicare, Medicaid, and many other entitlements as a way of slowing down the accumulation of more debt in our country. All along, under their breath these businessmen are laughing like hell because they're sending middle-class manufacturing jobs to slave labor countries or are invested in companies that do.. Not one time during the interviews will these businessmen admit to sending US manufacturing jobs to slave labor countries, because the news commentators won't ask the question. Are you involved in or invested in companies that out-source jobs to slave labor countries? Outsourcing jobs does affect the unemployed and underemployed in the United States. Don, if you think employment isn't affected by jobs being sent to slave labor countries, you better go back to college. These businessmen that give their opinions about the economy should also announce ahead of time whether or not they're involved with any companies that send US manufacturing jobs to slave labor countries.

Don we need your voice!

Eliminating the **"N"** word from the English language does not put food on the table or; put a nice roof over one's head. It doesn't eliminate poverty or crime or violence.

Jobs are our only way out!

Ross Perot

Ross Perot was born in Texarkana, Texas, attended the US Naval Academy, became a businessman starting Electronic Data Systems (EDS) founded in 1962. Eventually General Motors Corporation purchased EDS making Ross a billionaire. Ross Perot is best known for his run for president in 1992. During his run for the presidency one of his main goals was stopping the future outsourcing of American jobs to foreign countries. He is also known for the phrase **"Giant Sucking Sound"** when referring to the creation of NAFTA. Now we not only have NAFTA, but we have, poorly used tariffs, and unfair trade agreements with foreign countries that are making that" Giant Sucking Sound". This is being accomplished with the approval of our government and supported by the news media. With high unemployment and underemployed, Perot's prediction has come true. The biased news media called this the global economy. The only way this could be a global economy is if the US manufacturing workers could compete. The biased news organizations know American workers cannot work for slave labor wages, so calling this a fair global economy is the biggest scam since the beginning of time. With the biased press and the un-American international businessman working together it is difficult for the middle-class manufacturing worker to have his voice heard.

The voices of 1 million unemployed and underemployed Americans shouting from the tallest mountain **"we need jobs with dignity"** will never be heard because of the biased press. As the old saying goes these

Americans voices would be "whistling in the wind'. The press will air the grievances of their rich buddies concerning the 47% percent of the American public who receive government assistance, while all along these un-American business executives are denying the 47% percent a right to a decent job. Those 47% percent are hungering to give back to the US government in the form of Social Security taxes, income taxes, sales tax, state taxes, and much more. The elite few in the business community are denying the middle-class that opportunity.

Ross Perot, the middle-class manufacturing worker needs your voice. The destruction of the middle-class non-college-educated worker is in high gear and heading for a cliff. Having your voice heard during your 1992 run for the presidency was imperative. You bought half-hour slots on TV to inform the public of your vision for the United States. Part of that vision was eliminating NAFTA from the scenery. Your vision was well received and very informative to the voters of our country. This helped you increase your popularity with the public because they understood your platform and your honest sincerity toward the middle-class workers. At this time fair unbiased reporting from the news organizations doesn't exist. Trying to brainwash the middle-class into thinking their so-called global economy is good for the United States is what they do best. The tides of poverty along with the lack of compassion for the forgotten members of society that lives in the ghetto or crime-ridden areas have drifted out to sea far too long. Reversing the tides of poverty, crime, unemployment, and underemployment must start now. Bringing middle-class jobs back to our shores is the only way to lick this ongoing crisis. The only jobs plan that middle-class citizens should hear, is when are we going to repeal NAFTA and unfair trade agreements and implement effective tariffs? There is absolutely no other way to cure the unemployment and underemployment problem.

It's the right of each citizen of the United States to have an equal opportunity in the global job market to obtain a job. The press will try to convince the American public that there is not a crisis of unemployment and underemployment. The main problem that our government is experiencing is still part of the ongoing banking crisis. As mentioned earlier it may take decades to overcome the abuses by the banks. Not everyone has the opportunity or ability to receive a college education. The manufacturing jobs that the un-American international business executives are sending to foreign countries are the type of jobs held by non-college-educated citizens. The outsourcing of these jobs must stop now and they must be returned to this country. Ross Perot, you've stood up for the American middle-class in the past, **we are asking for your voice to be heard by the American people again**. It takes a special person or group of special people to expose big business and the unethical journalism that comes from our national news organizations. We must eliminate the one-sided journalistic view of our economy that the news organizations continue to ram down the throats of our US citizens must start now. The only way to fight jaded journalism is with a barrage of ads on national television stations exposing the global economy for what it is, **"that giant sucking sound"** of US jobs being outsourced to slave labor countries. Buying one minute announcements on TV denouncing the outsourcing of manufacturing jobs would go a long way toward opening the eyes of our leaders. We need to rally around someone who cares and has the willingness to step up and be heard. Poverty and crime can't be reversed without the opportunity to secure a decent job with dignity.

The crisis in the home building industry and the lack of incoming revenue to our treasury are exposed by the lack of jobs. The millions and millions of jobs that the United States has lost to slave labor countries in the past 10 to 12 years were good paying American manufacturing jobs that paid between$15 and $30 an hour. Our country has lost millions of potential homebuyers during the downturn of our economy. Our country needs a spokesperson for the millions of middle-class American workers. The rich have the news media in their back pockets, which means that hundreds of supporters of the rich having access to the airwaves.

PART I: ROSS PEROT

There is a TV spokesperson who expressed his thoughts concerning the poor, the disadvantage children, and the older retired people, whether they were in wheelchairs, on walkers, or were disabled veterans that fought in wars to maintain his freedom. Paraphrasing: He said: I'm rich, I'm special, and I don't need Social Security or Medicare. He said he wanted to keep his tax breaks no matter what the cost to our treasury or the middle-class. He feels he's that important. His opinion about how this could be accomplished was that it would require revisiting the middle-class entitlements such as Medicare, Medicaid, and Social Security with the goal of slashing their benefits so that he and his rich buddies could maintain their tax breaks. This is the mindset of the greedy rich, to hell with the children of poverty, to hell with the disabled veterans, to hell with the families living in shelters, to hell with the people that don't have the opportunity to obtain a job. He and his friends are already rich, but to enrich themselves more, they're not above walking on people and destroying their lives and their children's lives. So if you have footprints on your back and sore ribs, more than likely you've been dealing with Mitt Romney or his type.

Ross Perot is 83 as of June 2013. Ross, we hope you live forever, but chances are slim that's going to happen. What's more realistic is that the dirt nap is just around the corner. Do you have one good fight left in you? The middle-class needs a helping hand to expose the global economy for what it is, that **"Giant Sucking Sound"**. NAFTA and the unfair trade agreements are causing despair and sadness in many middle-class families and that and must stopped now. The influence of a man of your prominence and experience would go a long way towards altering the destruction of many middle-class families.

Ross Perot your country needs your help!
Ross Perot your country needs your voice to be heard!

Quote from Franklin Delano Roosevelt
"The best customer of American industry is the well-paid worker"

35

Oprah Winfrey

Oprah Winfrey is the most influential African-American woman in the twentieth and twenty-first centuries. She gained her fame while hosting a TV talk show. The Oprah Winfrey Show, her movie career, and the cable network OWN has made her a billionaire. Oprah is well known for her generous support of education. She's given scholarships to hundreds of African- Americans to help them continue their higher learning. It is a well-known fact that higher education for African-Americans changes the landscape of their lives. Most will receive jobs paying a wage that affords them the opportunity to prosper and become middle-class citizens. This enables them to leave behind the high- crime areas that are overrun with drugs and poverty. Looking back and being proud of what you have achieved is exciting, but your support for African-Americans, white, and Hispanic- Americans communities is not completed. A person who speaks out about discrimination and the injustices that the African-Americans have endured for centuries, is an admirable quality. If you watch TV or listen to the news, you know African-Americans are portrayed as criminals, high on crack, living in high crime areas riddled with poverty while living in section 8 housing and receiving handouts from the government.. This must change! These are the same unethical news agencies that are in bed with the un-American international business executives that send US jobs to slave labor countries and call this a global economy.

The despair of the African American worker is taking its toll on many minority families. After getting up in the morning having one's coffee or tea and getting ready to take on the world too often reality sets in. Outsourcing of American manufacturing jobs continue to create unfulfilled dreams and the desire to contribute to the family. Instead, glancing out the window he sees vacant buildings, buildings in need of repair, and buildings being demolished just for their scrap value. These buildings once house the future of many manufacturing workers and their families. Some of these buildings housed machine shops where lays, mills, and grinders, where the hub of activity. Some buildings housed molding machines that produced billions of plastic parts. Automotive parts, computer parts, everyday household items, even toys that our children use every day are mainly produced from plastic. Some of these buildings were homes for stamping presses. Automobile parts were the prime products of many stamping plants. The millions upon millions of parts for the automobile industry created millions of jobs throughout the United States. These barren and empty buildings housed the industries that once employed millions upon millions of American manufacturing workers that made this country great. Being the melting pot of the world African-Americans, white Americans, Hispanic Americans, and many other nationalities were employed in these industries. Now we have these un-American international CEOs supported by their boards of directors that feel these American employees are now expendable.

Many of our wealthy citizens have senators and representatives in their back pocket which makes it easy to understand why our American businesses and citizens are taking a backseat to foreign slave labor. Our Congressman have thrown the unemployed and the underemployed blacks, whites, Hispanics and many other nationalities under the bus so they can enrich themselves. Outsourcing manufacturing jobs affects the African-American society disproportionately because they have a larger percentage of non-college-educated citizens in their communities. The African-American community should be pounding the table about the injustices that are taking place in their communities. The racist un-American international executives of business are creating an unfair global economy that discriminates against US manufacturing workers. Global economy means everyone can compete. The African-American community would like a chance to achieve the middle-class life style so they can be role models for their children. To accomplish this we need **jobs jobs jobs jobs jobs !** Finding anyone in the US willing to work for $.50 to $2.50 an hour is going to be challenging. The brainwashing by the national news media, **(American job destroyers)** with the support of the un-American business executives is the biggest scam since the beginning of time. The transferring of US manufacturing jobs to slave labor countries affects all college and non college educated citizens. These companies need computer programmers, accountants, and many more college educated personnel. Unethical outsourcing effects all layers of our society.

The voices of the influential African-Americans, white Americans, and Hispanics Americans condemning the outsourcing of middle-class manufacturing jobs must start now. The children living in the slums, with high crime and poverty as a way of life deserve better. This atmosphere will never change unless we have jobs. Education is the best way to alter this revolving door, but after 60 years of trying, we need other alternatives. **There is absolutely no way to alter this lifestyle without jobs.**

Lately many influential African-Americans have been complaining about the excessive use of the "N" word and how it sheds a negative light on the African-American community. Very few people use the" N word", because it is unacceptable in most communities. But it does seem to be acceptable in the African-American community. A hundred years from now the "N-word" will still be in use. You're wasting your time beating a dead horse, it doesn't really matter. Removing the word "nigger" from the English language does not put food on the table, eliminate poverty, eliminate crime, or give a man a job with dignity. **Oprah, we need your voice**, condemning the transferring of American manufacturing jobs to third world countries that support slave labor wages.

Celebrities

We have many celebrities in this country, movie stars, singers, sports figures, or TV personalities. Many of the celebrities in the past and present have stepped forward and spoken out about the injustices in the world and in the United States. Some have put their careers on the line to expose these injustices. We have a crisis in this country that's destroying many American middle-class families. That crisis is the raping of the common man by un-American international business executives. NAFTA and unfair trade agreements must be repealed. Fair tariffs must be used to give the American workers a level playing field. Help is needed now! Your voices and faces are needed to expose the destruction of the American middle-class. Your voices need to be heard!

Just think of it. Of all the people born in this world, you are one of the lucky people to be born in the United States or to have immigrated to this country. There are approximately seven billion people in the world at this time and if you're one of the high profile figures I'm talking about, you are one of the few fortunate people to obtain superstar status in your field. Most of your struggles are easily recalled, the ups and downs of an unknown newcomer, along with rehearsals, going to try-outs, rejection after rejection, and the callbacks that never came. You've traveled your own road, but you have many things in common with others who've reached that kind of success you enjoy. Each person needs perseverance, determination, and the tireless effort put into achieving celebrity status. You may have been a waiter or waitress, or you may have worked in construction, hauled garbage, driven a cab or whatever needed to be done to achieve their goals.

The hard-working manufacturing employees are at a precarious position at this time. Their job future has been put on the fence by the passage of NAFTA and unfair trade agreements. The job prospects have been tipped over and are falling fast. America needs someone or some group to furnish a lifeline or the collapse of our manufacturing community is inevitable. Competing against employees in foreign countries that are working for slave wages and forgoing major health care benefits, unemployment benefits, Social Security benefits, Medicare benefits and much more is an impossible task.

Major health care benefits: Most American manufacturing companies furnish healthcare, so when going to a doctor, a small part of the total cost for the office visit is the responsibility of the employee. Being admitted to a hospital in the United States, an employee will receive some of the best medical care in the world. These medical benefits come at a high cost to the employer. In third world countries finding a local family doctor is very difficult and being admitted to a local hospital with adequate facilities is almost impossible. Most hospitals in third world countries are poorly furnished, and the staff is very seldom is fully educated. The Un-American executives that relocate American manufacturing jobs to third world countries have few medical costs if any. Having few medical obligations is a huge savings and adds to the company's bottom line.

Unemployment benefits: This is another cost that each employer must pay twice a year. In the United States being laid off from a job is not an automatic end to wages. The laid-off American employee is eligible for unemployment benefits, the amount of benefits is determined by the wages of each employee.

American workers on average are paid approximately 10 times more than their counterparts in third world countries, so the amount collected by laid-off American employees is considerably more than a third world country employee if they receive any unemployment compensation at all. In the United States, the state collects a percentage of each employer's payroll to cover the cost of the unemployment benefits. Companies that outsource American manufacturing jobs eliminate this cost adding more money to the company's bottom line.

Medicare benefits: These benefits are normally available to the retiree at the age of 65. These benefits cover part of the medical expenses that a elderly person may incur during the final years of his or her life. The federal government collects 7% percent of each employees pay to cover his costs. At different times the percentage has fluctuated but normally it's about 7% percent. The employer's obligation is also 7% percent. By moving American manufacturing jobs to slave labor countries eliminates the need for employers to pay another 7% percent of the employees wages. This is a giant savings to the un-American business executives. Just imagine how much money is lost to Medicare because of the millions and millions of jobs being sent to slave labor countries. Without NAFTA and unfair trade agreements Social Security and Medicare would be flush with money. The unethical one-sided journalism that the news media practices is creating a hell on earth for many middle-class families and their children.

Unemployment at this time hovers around 7% percent. This does not cover the millions upon millions of good honest hard-working manufacturing workers that are underemployed. There is only one reason why our country's employment picture has not rebounded and that's because the outsourcing of American manufacturing jobs to slave labor countries.

Celebrities, the American manufacturing employees need your voices! As you can see the American manufacturing worker is at a major disadvantage and this must change and change now. Please lend a helping voice, it's badly needed.

Judge Mathis

Judge Mathis is a TV personality along with being a self made man. By his own account, he was once part of the crime scene in Detroit Michigan. After dropping out of school, Greg Mathis spent time on the streets of Detroit selling drugs. Greg was arrested numerous times which took him through the juvenile court system. Eventually the court system came to the end of the line with Greg and offered him one last chance before going to jail. Getting his GED and holding a job were among the conditions for his release. Greg Mathis changed his ways, got his GED, attend college, becoming a lawyer, and then became a judge. You have to applaud him for changing his life and becoming a model citizen.

Being a popular celebrity on television gives him an opportunity to voice his opinion on different subjects. His specialty at this time is encouraging the under educated middle-class to get special training because having a GED or high school diploma is not enough in this day and age.

Judge Mathis I guess when you became rich and famous you forget how things were when you were younger. Many of your former friends and their children lived in impoverished areas with little chance of a future which many times leads to crime and prison. To expect the millions of people that have GED's and high school diplomas to get higher education or a trade is unrealistic.

It wasn't too long ago that having a GED or high school diploma opened doors in the manufacturing community, offering an opportunity to obtain a job with dignity and fair wages. It wasn't as good as having a a college degree, but it put an honest, middle-class way of life in sight.

Big business pushed for and received unfair trade agreements and NAFTA along with the support of many news organizations and Congress. Since these agreements have taken effect having a GED or high school diploma isn't good enough because manufacturing jobs have been sent to Mexico, China, India, Vietnam, and many other countries. **Is this what you call an even playing field for US middle-class manufacturing workers?**

Judge Mathis has said many times on television that the poor must get better educations, If this is not possible they should hold two or three jobs. A large percentage of homes in poor neighborhoods have a single parent as the head of the household, usually the woman. Who's home supervising the children while she works 2 or 3 jobs to support the family? With unsupervised children living at home while the single parent is out working extra jobs, are we not putting these children on the open market toward juvenile delinquency. **Judge, the country needs your voice.** Judge, since you've become rich I imagine you and your family have visited Disney World, the beach, or have traveled throughout the world. Look around at how many patrons are minorities. I guess having 2 or 3 jobs still doesn't afford them a reasonable middle-class life.

It is sad to say that many people who become rich, get blindsided by money and forget how their life began. Judge Mathis, we need help! How are we going to change this cycle of the poor not having an opportunity for a middle-class life? If jobs aren't available how are the children of the next generation going to escape the violence and poor lifestyles. Without jobs available, what's to be done with the 47% percent that receive government assistance? In the international business community, having a conscience has developed into a dirty word. Having that little voice acting as a guide that tells one the difference between right and wrong is missing. Business executives that have a conscience would be putting their country first instead of gaining wealth through the destruction of the families in the US manufacturing communities.

A business executive with a conscience would want to repeal NAFTA and the unfair trade agreements and would welcome the use of effective tariffs that would give our manufacturing community and opportunity to compete in a global world. Being able to compete in a global world would be the vehicle to reach the middle-class society. If an American manufacturing employee was put on par with foreign workers I'm sure there would be a huge demand for their services. Having a demand for their services would eventually dismantle the destruction of the wage base of the manufacturing worker.

At the end of each TV show we need celebrities to speak out against **NAFTA and unfair trade agreements and for the use of effective tariffs** to give our manufacturing workers an opportunity to compete in a global world.

There are many people that came from poor or underprivileged backgrounds that have achieved great success in life. Along with the success came money, power, and privilege. The people that have found success in this country and who love this country have a moral obligation to assist the discarded middle-class manufacturing employee in regaining prominence in our communities..

Driving through many parts of the United States you can see empty buildings with boards covering the glassless Windows and grass growing up the walls of the discarded structures. These grand buildings once house machinery that was used in producing everyday goods. The quiet that surrounds these buildings now produce an eerie silence. Where is the hustle and bustle of the employees before the opening bell sounds or when shift change takes place. **Where are the American workers that made this country great?** The American manufacturing worker has been discarded, thrown away like a used doll or broken toy. But they are a continued source of laughter to many of the news commentators, the greedy rich, and the un-American international CEOs of business along with their boards of directors. They have a famous saying "screw the little guy". These people are picking the skin off the bones and devouring the human spirit for survival of many of our cherished citizens. Without the opportunity for jobs the only thing left to do is join the 47% percent on government assistance.

The laughter of the international business community along with many news commentators echoes through the halls of the grand banquet suites. The main theme of laughter and ridicule revolves around the **stupidity** of the American middle-class worker. The CEOs and boards of directors believe anyone that thinks paying foreign employees between $.50 and $2.50 an hour in slave labor countries and calling this a global economy is good for America is, an **idiot**. Behind closed doors, they thank the national news organizations **(American job destroyers)** for their help in brainwashing the American public into supporting an unfair global economy.

Judge Mathis we need you to speak out and condemn the raping of your country and its citizens by the un-American international business community.

Being a virgin onlooker in our court system can be a very sad and disheartening experience. Our courts are filled with under educated, unemployed, underemployed, and abused defendants. Most coming from broken homes with nonworking parents or single parent families with poor lifestyles. Through no fault of their own, their future was mapped out very early in their life. I imagine the judges and lawyers become hardened and less sympathetic to the traffic that flows through their courts.

Watching the different court shows on television you eventually become accustomed to the lifestyles of many of the plaintiffs and defendants.

Large portions of the litigants that appear on these shows are poor, under educated, unemployed, and underemployed. You can tell by their use of the English language that many of the litigant's education was less than adequate. While presenting their case many times it comes to the attention of the judge that some of the litigants are part of Mitt Romney's 47% percent receiving government assistance. Many of the litigants that are on government assistance seem healthy and strong.

45

There have been times where the judge has become a little frustrated and short because in the judge's mind they feel our tax dollars are being wasted. Judge Mathis, you should be more upset at the greedy criminals in the banking industry that have yet to be prosecuted. The un-American business executives that have outsourced jobs that your unemployed and underemployed litigants would love to have, and the biased press that supports an unfair global economy. I have sympathy for many of your litigants because I've seen many do well in the manufacturing industry and are good high school educated people but would probably struggle in college. But they still have the mechanical skills to be good employees in the manufacturing industry. The frustration of these young people that want a job is heartbreaking. These citizens are eager for employment and would gladly do whatever is necessary to achieve employment. They just want a decent job! Some of these people have been denied a job for so long they become lost souls and have just given up hope. I have seen what happens to some people that have tried and tried to gain employment,, bitterness and hatred against society takes over. A lack of confidence sets in and some turn to crime. Starting out as good honest citizens, now they have become part of the criminal element in society. It's better that they are part of Mitt Romney 47% percent than getting caught in the revolving door of criminal activity.

Judge, we need your voice condemning the outsourcing of American manufacturing jobs **our economy must be balanced, with jobs for college educated and non-college citizens. The African-American community, white community, Hispanic community, needs your voice condemning the outsourcing of American manufacturing jobs.** When the direction of our country changes, your courtroom will have less of Mitt Romney's 47% percent receiving government assistance. There is absolutely no other way.

In the past few years our prisons population have exploded, and the majority of the prisoners are African-American. Without having the opportunity to secure employment we can tell which way they turned, drugs and crime. After coming out of prison which way does a paroled person turn? If jobs were unavailable before they had a prison record how are they going to secure employment now? With little chance of getting a job, the cycle of crime and violence will eventually send them back to jail. The vicious cycle starts all over again. The devastation of the African-American community, the white community, the brown community, and all others is taking place, just so a few rich un-American international business executives can become richer

Judge we need your voice!

Unions

"Unions" at one time was a respectable word. Belonging to a union gave you security, a living wage, and the road to a middle-class life. Through the years unions has turned into a dirty word. CNN and many TV news organizations portray the unions as job killers. Of course the news outlets won't talk about the millions upon millions of jobs that have been sucked out of the United States in the name of global economy. The only job killers in the United States are the un-American news networks that support the un-American international business executives that own our congressmen and women. The union leaders of the past are not just turning over in their graves they are spinning. Organizers from the 20s, 30s, 40s and 50s who were beaten up in back alleys, fired from their jobs, some paid the ultimate price with their lives to give the middle-class and opportunity to prosper. Business owners constantly clashed with employees that wanted safe working environments and a living wage. Losing a hand, finger, or arm in a press was not an uncommon experience. Many employees died an early death because of breathing fumes or dust particles that business owners knew were toxic. OSHA, was born out of the disregard that business owners had for their employees. During negotiations with big business, unions demanded safety equipment be installed to protect the employees. Big business CEOs and board members fought against these safety precautions because it slowed down production. Big business felt it was more important to maintain production than for the safety of their employees. They claimed that if OSHA went through it would bankrupt their companies. The federal government had to drag them kicking, screaming into the world of worker safety, OSHA was established. As usual big business was lying and with OSHA in the forefront the safety of the American workers were protected.

The EPA was born out of big business's disregard for the environmental safety of their employees. In the early years toxic waste was dumped in the rivers and streams that were adjacent to their businesses. This toxic waste eventually polluted and destroyed the fish and wildlife that was in the waterways and killed the nearby animals. Many farmers had to stop using those streams and rivers as a source of drinking water for their livestock which was eventually deemed undrinkable. Many families had their wells condemned because the polluted water found its way into their source of drinking water. Dumping toxic waste on the grounds was not an uncommon practice. When many of these companies eventually shut down their property was condemned as unfit for any use. The business executives knew the waste that they were dumping in the rivers, streams, and on the land was toxic. Not one time has the executives of these companies ever owned up to the destruction of the land and rivers. Now big business is trying to sell the American workers another basket of rotten apples. Big business CEOs are standing on a pulpit professing that an unfair global economy is good for the United States. The scam of the century, which affects all Americans citizens continues to roll.

The purpose of a union is to represent their members in negotiations with management, during negotiations the discussion of working conditions, wages, health care benefits, and retirement benefits that supplements Social Security helping with the transition to old age. God forbid if you get laid off, but some unions have negotiated a supplement to unemployment benefits to help members through the hard times. Having a wage structure that allows you to live an honorable Middle-class life style is also discussed.

Receiving a pay structure with a future is not the goal of the greedy rich un-American international business community, their goal is to have the American manufacturing worker grovel at the feet of the rich.

Before you know it the news networks are going to say that kissing the feet of rich CEOs is good for America. It's about time the American worker learns his place!

Through the years the unions have become weak, disorganized, and have sold out to big business. When jobs started going south to Mexico the weakness of the union surfaced. Why the unions didn't fight harder when NAFTA was proposed is beyond me. There is absolutely no benefit to the American worker having their jobs moved to slave labor countries. How can American worker making between $15 and $30 an hour with benefits compete with foreign workers making between $.50 and $2.50 an hour? Is there no common sense left in this country? When NAFTA was first proposed there were very few people vehemently against this from taking place. One such person was Ross Perot. **Our country needs the voice of Ross Perot again.**

Since the passage of NAFTA, poorly used tariffs, and the unfair trade agreements have become active, the wage structure for middle-class American workers has **collapsed**. This is exactly what big business and the international business community are anticipating. Years ago this was one of the strategies put forward by the business executives, to move American jobs to third world countries creating a glut of unemployed and underemployed American workers. When a company posts a job opening there are between 40 to 60 and as much as 1000 applicants for that one job. With the collapse of the American wage structure many manufacturing jobs now pay between $8 to $13 an hour along with reduced benefits. The greedy international business community can thank NAFTA and the unfair trade agreements for slowly turning parts of America into another third world country. The United States has one of the largest ghetto population in the world.

Much of this has taken place because the unions have turned over and are playing dead. The union leaders are old and have lost the vision for the future of their members. Their past union leaders once had heart and love for their union members. No one's looking for wild strikes, just an effort to turn back the un-American international business community from destroying our country from within.

Where are the organizations that are actively trying to repeal NAFTA, the unfair trade agreements, or using an effective tariff system to create a level playing field for US workers? The unions have the money and the ability to fight for the American middle-class worker. They should step up because it's the right thing to do, not because it would increase their membership the American middle-class worker needs help.

The AFL CIO, Teamsters, UAW, and other unions say they are concerned about the global trade and economic conditions. Their concerns have not turned into action, American middle-class workers need help!

By the lack of commitment and not putting forth an effort all union members are putting their jobs in jeopardy. You could be next. All union workers should refuse to pay union dues. This should continue until the unions start putting pressure on the right people to repeal NAFTA and unfair trade agreements. The union members must fight back. With the wage structure having collapsed, union workers **wages** are in further jeopardy of being reduced and the request by management for another pay reduction is not too far in the future. Even a pay cut will not protect you from the unfair labor practices that take place in slave labor countries. When your job leaves the country and your middle-class way of life is jeopardized, it may be too late. Obtaining a level playing field for American workers and having a balanced work force(employment for non-college educated as well as college-educated workers) is not going to be easy so you must start now. Big business leaders not only laugh and make fun of American middle-class workers, unions workers are next on their list.

The unions hire strategists to advise them on how to handle different situations. The rank-and-file union members are wasting their money if the strategist's pay scale is more than a dollar a day. The unions must take charge and explore different options that exist today in enhancing their reputation.

The union leaders expose their misunderstanding of the US economy and lack of caring for their union members by not aggressively opposing the transfer of US manufacturing jobs. This takes place when unions support candidates running for Congress that say: outsourcing jobs to slave labor countries is good for America, the jobs lost to foreign countries will never return to the United States, and repealing NAFTA and the free-trade agreements is not going to happen. These candidates also express their lack of concern for union members by laughing and making fun of the stupidity of union members.

If these candidates are quizzed on whether the outsourced jobs will ever return to US soil, their standard answer is no, and outsourcing of jobs is good for our country. Even though millions upon millions of jobs have been outsourced by uncaring business executives, this trend has not been completed. Crippling our manufacturing workforce is the objective of big business. In doing so demanding reduced pay and less benefits, is there main goal. Each manufacturing worker should encourage their local union leaders to support all efforts to repeal NAFTA and unfair trade agreements. A legitimate tariff placed on incoming goods to provide middle-class manufacturing workers with a level playing field should also be encouraged. A standard theme should echo through all union halls:

We need jobs!

NAFTA and unfair trade agreements must go!

The only candidates supported by the unions must include a platform where outsourcing jobs is not acceptable and the repeal of NAFTA and unfair trade agreements is the candidate's main agenda.

In the year 2009 General Motors was on the verge of collapse as the final outcome of bankruptcy was in the wind. The citizens of the United States came to the rescue with billions of dollars of taxpayers money to assist in the bailout. With the US bailout money in hand, expanding in Mexico was a high priority item. General Motors has decided to invest approximately $1 billion in Mexico and 200 million in the United States. A new transmission plant is planned for Mexico along with the assembly of the Chevy Silverado truck and the GM Sierra. After assembly of these vehicles is completed at slave labor wages it's easy to drive across the border tariff free. Without NAFTA and the free-trade agreements, this would be an impossible task.

I guess the United States general public gets the one finger wave from the General Motors executives.

General Motors is not the only car company doing business in Mexico. Every automotive manufacturer that sells cars in the US is also manufacturing cars in Mexico or is planning to in the near future. Bringing these cars tariff free in the United States is destroying the wage base of US manufacturing workers.

Small Businesses

All small businesses should examine their federal taxes that the government collects each year. Compare them to the many large corporations and you will notice the percentage of taxes on small businesses is much greater than larger corporations. The opportunity for small businesses to hide their profits in foreign countries is almost nonexistent.

Over the past few years some large corporations have paid few taxes if any at all. Because of operating in foreign countries, most large corporations have the luxury of avoiding large portions of US taxes. Many of the CEOs of these large corporations make millions and millions of dollars each year. That's not enough. They attack the middle-class because of their so-called entitlements. The United States international business community doesn't feel it is right, as middle-class ages they receive Social Security along with Medicare. These CEOs feel these entitlements should be abolished or at lease cut to the bone. Eliminating Social Security and Medicare along with subsidize housing for the poor and many more entitlements would help cut the US debt. The lack of jobs and getting old is not the governments problem. Executives of many large corporations sit back and laugh at the American middle-class. Brainwashing is easy with the help of the TV news organizations, this is the global economy at work.

At this time big business is pushing for the tax code to be overhauled. If taking a new look at the tax code is to lower taxes on big business you are being scammed again. The top 200 corporations in this country have an average tax burden of around 17percent. Many of the CEOs of large corporations promise the revitalization of jobs in this country if their taxes are lowered. These CEOs just lie. In 2004 US corporations had over $300 billion tucked away in foreign countries. They promised jobs would be created if allowed to bring the $300 billion back to the United States at a reduced tax rate.

A grace period on taxes was granted and the money flowed back to the United States at a reduced rate. Out of that $300 billion not one job was created not one. Many of these corporations were outsourcing jobs while claiming they would create jobs in United States. The un-American CEOs of these multinational companies just laughed at the stupidity of our country. If the CEOs of these corporations pants caught on fire every time they lied someone would have to follow them around with a fire extinguisher. It's understandable why many citizens that are struggling to make ends meet in this troubled economy want to believe these lying CEOs. Exposing the CEOs and their lying ways is very difficult. The organizations that are available to expose the biased press and the unscrupulous business people are disorganized and poorly funded.

Before the Civil War many states in the South had slaves, this was eventually abolished in the United States. Throughout the world, however, alarmingly low wages reduce people to the level of slavery. Slave wages are still a very common practice in Mexico, China, India, and all third world countries.

The CEOs and boards of directors of these multinational companies are the new masters of slaves. The slave owners of old used to house, clothe, and feed their slaves. If the old-time slaves caused the slightest problem the masters would have them **flogged** to maintain order. The new masters are smarter, their goal is to pay the new slaves just enough money to clothe and feed themselves. When these new slaves complete work, they go to a place they call home. Many of these homes look like the shacks that the American slaves occupied before the Civil War. Most third world shacks are occupied by many people and families. Not much different than the slaves of the old South. Most floggings have been outlawed so if an employee of these multinational corporations has a thought of their own, they are fired. With the overpopulation of many third world countries it's easy to hire a new slave. **This is the global economy at work.** Many of these corporations have been in Third World countries for 30, 40, 50 years, all along claiming their employees will eventually become consumers. Thirty years ago starting pay at that time was approximately $.25 an hour, now 40 years later these employees pay has skyrocketed to $.75 to one dollar an hour. At that rate of pay becoming a consumer is very difficult.

The people of the United States must be honest with themselves. These executives of large corporations will say anything to convince you that they are trustworthy, but liar is their middle name. Giving these corporations more tax breaks will never, never, never bring one manufacturing job back to the United States. When companies transfer American jobs to slave labor countries, dealing with OSHA, EPA, workman's comp, job discrimination, lawyers, state taxes, city taxes, sales taxes, corporate taxes, Social Security tax, income taxes, is no longer a problem.

Big business claims:

(1) Since Social Security was introduced into Congress and that passing Social Security would be the first step toward socialism, it wasn't the government's job to assist old people, and Social Security would bankrupt this country.
(2) When Medicare was introduced into Congress, they claimed that assisting old people with healthcare would bankrupt this country.
(3) They claimed that unemployment benefits for laid-off workers would bankrupt their companies.
(4) They claim they didn't pollute the rivers and streams that ran near their businesses.
(5) They claimed they did not dump toxic waste on the land and making it unusable for generations to come.

(6)   The tobacco companies claimed smoking their product would not cause an early death nor was it addictive.

This is just the tip of the iceberg.

Big business just lies!

The un-American national news organizations(**American job destroyers**) fail to discuss

(1)   The amount of money foreign slaves are paid.

(2)   The amount of foreign government assistance that is given to American businesses that relocate to their countries.

(3)   How many jobs have been outsourced in the past 10 to 15 years.

(4)   The millions of small businesses that have been destroyed by outsourcing American jobs.

(5)   Where would our country be if jobs had not been outsourced in the past 10 to 15 years..

(6)   The destruction of the wage base for manufacturing workers.

(7)   When talking about high unemployment and underemployment why is job outsourcing not discussed.

(8)   How badly Chicago's African-American community need jobs to change this cycle of poverty, crime, and a lack of a future for their children, like most of the communities in the United States.

(9)   That the United States needs a balanced workforce, college-educated and non-college-educated jobs.

(10)   **Why CNN and the national news organizations (American job destroyers)** favor the rich.

Exploring these issues and many more by CNN and the news organizations is nonexistent.

These children's future is in jeopardy because small businesses that are the backbone of our country are closing daily because of NAFTA and unfair trade agreements

The national news organizations say small businesses are the backbone of our country and economy. Yet small manufacturing businesses are closing every day in the United States. At one time there were hundreds of thousands of small businesses throughout this great country which dotted the horizon everywhere. With the large amount of small business closings, eventually the small manufacturing businesses are going to appear on the government's endangered species list. The government protects the bald eagle from extinction but protecting the small businesses and their employees from extinction doesn't seem to be a priority. At one time the news media stated that, we need the small business entrepreneurs to help lead us out of this employment crisis. Eventually the entrepreneurs that dream of opening their own small manufacturing business will also appear on the government's endangered species list. Competing against the US governments assessment of a level playing field kills the American entrepreneurial spirit. The small businesses that are left needs to fight back, because you may be next.. Taking out ads in the newspaper, radio, and television condemning the direction in which our country is taking is a must. Organizing, and opposing any politician that does not demand that our government reassess their commitment to unfair trade policies needs to start now. This is a must for our country to move forward in a positive direction.

Mitt Romney

Mitt Romney's life started on March 12, 1947, the son of George W Romney who at one time threw his hat in the ring hoping to become President of the United States. Mitt Romney was raised in the lap of wealth and luxury, enjoying the life of the super rich. Mitt Romney has never had to stand in line to collect unemployment benefits, food stamps or stand in line so his family could receive a meal in soup kitchens. He never had to live in a shelter, or live in section 8 housing and receive assisted living payments from the government. Yet this special human being says he understands how the unemployed, underemployed, and poor people feel and live.

Mitt Romney, while running for president of the United States opened the doors of his life so the future voters would be able to take a glimpse of this man as a human being. It seemed like during the campaign that the voters became disenchanted with his so-called religious values. Mitt Romney claimed to carry God in his heart but to the voters of this country it seemed like his true God is the Almighty dollar. It's difficult for the average citizen to believe Mitt Romney has true religious values when his wealth has been enhanced by the destruction of hundreds if not thousands of his former employees lives.

The voters were given the opportunity to explore the true person Mitt Romney had really become. The purpose of shutting down businesses and outsourcing jobs was for one reason and one reason only, slave labor in third world countries.

This has caused the destruction of the lives of many middle-class manufacturing workers at his plants. Outsourcing jobs to slave labor countries was just a vehicle so he and his family could become richer. When Mitt gets into his new overpriced car, takes exotic vacations, takes his boat out on a pleasure cruise, or goes skiing, does he hear the cries of his former employees children. Remember Mitt you are living off former employees that have had homes repossessed, cars repossessed and children that had their childhood taken from them. How many former employees lost their health insurance that caused an early death in the family? How many of your former employees thought of committing suicide because they lacked the opportunity to support their families? Mitt Romney, you held in your hands, the lives of hundreds of your former employees that did not want to become part of Mitt's 47% percent. They just wanted a job.

It's important that the citizens of the United States understand how business executives like you think. Did you not say: workers in the United States must compete in the global economy? I imagine your former employees and every other person in the United States would love to hear from you on how they can raise a family on $.50 to $2.50 an hour with few benefits. Mitt, how do you sleep at night knowing that you created a living hell for the children of these displaced workers. How many Christmas holidays have you ruined for these children? How many unfulfilled dreams have these children lost, just so you can have more.

Mitt, you've shown the world what kind of man you really are, creating a situation where your former employees receive unemployment benefits, welfare benefits, food stamps, and other assistances from the government. Then attending meetings with your rich Associates and complain about 47% percent receiving government assistance, a situation that you have created for thousands of your former employees. Comparing you to the lowest form of life on earth is giving the lowest form of life a bad name.

We have seen Mitt Romney in action, closing down plants, causing chaos in your former employee's lives, turning a deaf ear to the cries of the children who have lost everything. Instead of destroying lives your energy should be redirected toward the creation of a strong middle-class.

The repeal of NAFTA and the unfair trade agreements along with using effective tariffs should be the new direction your life now takes. During the Thanksgiving holidays, a picture of you and your family was displayed on television. Another one-sided showing of jaded journalism! Displaying the Thanksgiving picture of one of Mitt Romney's displaced workers was not forthcoming. Their Thanksgiving probably took place at the local soup kitchen. The companies and lives that you and your business Associates have destroyed would not have taken place without NAFTA and the unfair trade agreements along with poorly used tariffs.

We need jobs, not lies, not promises, not distortions, the middle-class manufacturing workers need jobs!

Teachers

The backbone of this country has always been our teachers. They are the captains of their classes, the champions of each pupil that attends their class. When a group of community leaders gather together, part of that group will contain teachers. In any endeavor that the community takes up the teachers are always in the forefront, asking how can they help. Most of the time they are the leaders or at worst an assistant to the leaders in their communities. Their hard work and toiless efforts are always appreciated. When a student is having difficulty with a subject, the majority of the time the teacher is at their side asking, how can I help. They will stay after school(without pay) to assist a student through a difficult time with a subject. If it's needed, coming in early is not a problem, whatever it takes to get the student through a rough spot in class. Many times a teacher becomes an advisor to students, because the divorce rate is up, unemployment up, and lack of money has taken root in many households. Because of these troubled times many students call on their favorite teachers for guidance and friendship. The student knows whatever is said in confidence will not be on the lips of other teachers or be the rumor traveling the hallways of the school. A special teacher has a big shoulder to cry on, not so much for a student to tell all but a caring teacher that has heard it all.

Being a teacher is not just about pulling out a book and hoping the student understands the subject, instead every effort is put forward to make sure that each student succeeds.

Now our teachers are under fire! The economy crisis is leading to the demands from many school districts for as much as 20% percent cut in pay and forgoing any raises for as much as five years. Extending the workday for many teachers is another option school districts are discussing. All the efforts that the local school districts have made through the years to develop a good loyal and stable workforce for their children is slowly disappearing. With the lack of money coming into many school districts the choices are few. The school board's burden of finding a way to balance the budget at this time falls on the teacher shoulders. The usual way to balance the school district's budget is requesting tax increases from the local residents. Most are small and easily pass. Through the years most residents receive pay raises from their job and are eager to help the school districts maintain high standards. The administrators of the local schools have had their fingers on the pulse of their community and understand many residents are laid off, have taken a pay cut, or have jobs that do not pay a living wage. At this time, local tax levies that support the school systems are not a priority to many residents, so failure of school levies are inevitable. There is only one reason for the backsliding of the middle-class and that is the international business executives that are sending American jobs to slave labor countries with the support of the unethical press and our US government.

The United States has lost millions and millions of jobs and is in the process of losing millions more. The words "U.S. manufacturing jobs" will eventually become a foreign phrase. While this transfer of jobs is taking place, what's to become of the children of these displaced workers? Most American employees are paid a reasonable income that affords them a middle-class way of life. So seeing firsthand the despair that many children face when income is lost is not something most working families see every day. But the teachers in many of these communities have to adjust to the heartbreaking emotions they experience each day. Not being able to control the sadness they experience is taking a toll on many of our good educators. We need the voices of our teachers, because they see every day the unfulfilled happiness that many of their students are experiencing. The outsourcing of manufacturing jobs must stop and change direction. A strong tariff system must be reinstated now.

Governors and mayors!

Many states and cities have been struggling to balance their budgets in the face of lagging revenues. The governors and mayors eventually do balanced their budgets, but at what cost to the American taxpayer? Some governors and mayors have raised sales tax and income tax to help balance their budgets. Some states have asked city and state workers to take a pay cut. Some states have demanded that teachers take a pay cut. The majority of the cuts have come by governors cutting funding for education, healthcare, police services, fire services, and human services. There are many other solutions being tried throughout our home states and cities. As the governors and mayors cut funding for different services the shortfall lands squarely on the shoulders of the American middle-class. Many governors want to blame the unions because state workers, city workers, and teachers, in their eyes are overpaid and receiving unfair pensions.

The governors should open up their eyes and put the blame where it belongs. Each Governor should reveal to the general public how many jobs were sent to slave labor countries. Checking this and furnishing the findings to the general public is easy. The US government has services that furnish these statistics.

A large portion of the governors are in bed with the multinational businesses that are destroying our country. The CEOs of many of these international companies have little or no loyalty to the United States.

PART I: GOVERNORS AND MAYORS!

In the past 10 to 15 years the United States has lost millions upon millions of jobs. Every time a governor speaks of high unemployment and an unbalanced budget they should inform the public, that these issues are not the fault of the teacher's salaries or the public employees pension funds. The governors and mayors know the real culprits are the un-American big business executives.

The problem is that governors and mayors know that being reelected without the help of big business's support and their money would be a difficult if not impossible undertaking. Money is the biggest influence on the outcome of most elections. With money the politicians can outspend their opponents who are seeking public office. Lying and twisting the truth is not above these public officials. Eliminating the truth in most elections seems to be common place and accepted by the majority of the public. The public must demand that outright lies and the twisting of the truth by our public officials must be eliminated from the campaigns for public office. CNN anointed themselves as the "fact checkers" of public officials 's running for office. After following CNN on their poor interpretation of the global economy, we need "fact checkers" to explore why CNN fails to discuss the abuses by their friends, the executives of big business.

The international business executives have bullied the governors and mayors into being cowards. Informing their citizens of jobs lost and future jobs to be lost to foreign countries has been buried in their negative propaganda condemning the teachers, police officers, firefighters, and anybody connected to unions. The unions have become the sacrificial lambs for the governors and mayors when reporting on the shortfalls of revenue that each state and city are experiencing. Having weak leadership in the unions has condemned them to a lifetime of ridicule. Standing up to the governors and mayors is the only way unions can regain their integrity. They must inform their members and American citizens of what's happening to manufacturing jobs in this great country. The government furnishes the statistics on what percentage of jobs have been outsourced from each state. It's an easy way to bring back respectability to the unions unless the union leaders are in bed with big business.

Each state has hotels, motels, restaurants, theaters, grocery stores, clothing outlets, car dealerships, homebuilders, remodelers, department stores, drugstores, and many other businesses that offer services to the middle-class. Not only have we lost millions of jobs to slave labor countries, but this migration has cost millions of jobs that were supported by those outsourced jobholders. Losing those millions upon millions of patrons has not only cost companies that offer services to the middle-class billions of dollars, but it has also cost the U.S. Treasury trillions of dollars. These manufacturing workers paid state income tax, federal income tax, sales tax, Social Security tax, real estate tax, school tax for education, and much more to support our economy. This money is lost because of poor leadership from our governors and mayors.

Governors, mayors, and small business owners must stand up and let your voices be heard!

We need voices of just one mayor or one governor to speak out and condemn the outsourcing of middle-class jobs to slave labor countries. Are all the mayors and governors unsympathetic to the families and their children living in poverty and in high crime areas. Look around at the people you promised to represent. Some are college educated and some are high school educated, but each person needs an opportunity to secure employment. Having an equal opportunity to prosper and raise our families with dignity, not the handouts of the 47% from the government but having the chance to give back to the government and community in the form of Social Security taxes, income taxes, sales taxes, state taxes, city taxes, school tax, and much more. Without jobs this can never happen.

Our governors and mayors need to speak out supporting the forgotten middle-class. Open up your hearts and listen to the cries of the children whose future lives are in jeopardy. Look around at the prosperity you and your family have accomplished. Without a job many of these children are doomed to a life of poverty and crime. By not speaking out, many of our governors and mayors are contributing to the downfall of the manufacturing workers and middle-class communities. The destruction of the United States is not going to come from an invasion by a foreign country, but from the lack of common sense from within. We need voices from some rich businessmen of this country exposing the global economy for what it is, the destruction of manufacturing jobs of the middle-class.

We need voices speaking out for the unemployed and underemployed who desperately need a level playing field when it comes to jobs. Mitt Romney, while running for president, you informed the people that you knew how to create jobs and turn this country around. Please, Mitt Romney, don't keep this knowledge to yourself, help your country and the Middle-class prosper again. Or were you just sending the poor unemployed and underemployed American people false hope while you send American middle-class jobs to slave labor countries. We need help. Turn back the future of poverty and crime for many of our non-college-educated citizens.

Our United States citizens needs jobs, jobs, jobs, jobs, jobs, jobs, jobs, jobs!

Mike Bloomberg

Mike Bloomberg, Mayor of New York City is one of the richest men in the world. Mike Bloomberg is a famous business man along with being an accomplished politician. Mayor Bloomberg is one of those politicians that believe in free trade. Unfair trade agreements contributed to the destruction of millions upon millions of American families' lives. Any person that believes sending American jobs that pay between $15-$30 an hour in the states to slave labor countries that pay between $.50 to $2.50 an hour and that's good for the United States has a few wires crossed.

Does Mayor Bloomberg profit from the destruction of our middle-class families? Does Mayor Bloomberg have investments in the companies that profit from outsourcing American manufacturing jobs? Any person that promotes the outsourcing of American manufacturing jobs should announce whether he or she is profiting from that practice. Look around Mayor, your support for unfair trade has caused the explosion of our prison systems, your support for unfair trade has caused the destruction of millions of middle-class families, Mayor your support for unfair trade has caused the destruction of the wage base of middle-class manufacturing workers, and much, much, more. Do your city a favor. Drive through the poor sections of your city, drive through the white sections, African-American sections, or Hispanics sections, and see how badly they need jobs. Many of the citizens of New York City are part of Mitt Romney's 47% percent receiving government assistance.

Supporting unfair trade agreements gives the impression that the unemployed and the underemployed citizens are expendable. As you're driving through the streets of the poor, keep your eyes open and refrain from nodding off.

Then you may notice the children of these families. What future do the children have when people like yourself are in power? You're looking at the future revolving door, poverty is not going to change, eliminating crime is never going to happen, and altering the drug scene is impossible without jobs. Mayor Bloomberg, you and your international business friends along with the biased press has mapped out these children's lives. Mayor Bloomberg your unfair trade stance along with the unfair global economy has destroyed any future these children have. Mayor Bloomberg if you support NAFTA, unfair trade agreements, and the non-use of effective tariffs, you support the slow destruction of the middle-class families. Mayor Bloomberg you should give a press conference announcing that you and your business associates have created millions of jobs so US citizens can compete in the global economy. When this happens you will become one of the most revered citizens in this country. Remind the future global economy employees, they should be proud to work for $.50 to $2.50 an hour with few benefits because that's the only way the US citizens can compete in your unfair global economy. The return of US jobs to our shores should be exciting news.

Mayor Bloomberg wants to stop selling large containers of pop to the public, but not once has the middle-class heard him condemn the outsourcing of middle-class manufacturing jobs. It's sad that Mayor Bloomberg feels a container of pop is more important than a man and his family's future.

Please Mr. Bloomberg, try and put a man's dignity and the well-being of his family as important as a container of pop. Speak out against the destruction of the middle-class that you and your international business friends are creating in this country. If the American people had an honest press, at least the middle-class would know they're being scammed, instead they are being brainwashed by the biased press. The international business executives, their families and the press laugh at the slaves in foreign countries because of their economic status. Affording a large soda is out of the question. Of course they are not overweight. A balanced economy, with college-educated along with non-college-educated citizens should have an opportunity to secure a job that pays a living wage. Strong and effective tariffs could put America on the right track so the citizens of our country can prosper again.

Mayor Bloomberg, I hope you hear the cries of the children that you and your business associates have condemned to a life of poverty and crime. The middle-class needs jobs, not more greedy businessmen.

Mayor Bloomberg considers himself a philanthropist. The word means "love of humanity," along with his private donations for public good focusing on the quality of life. Anyone that benefits from sending American jobs to slave labor countries that are destroying this country's manufacturing community is lacking a real heart, soul, and compassion one needs to become a true philanthropist. Mayor Bloomberg walks around with his chest out and his gums flapping, proclaiming he is a great human being, is he making billions of dollars through the destruction of non-college-educated American citizens lives? While driving through the poor sections of New York, does Mayor Bloomberg laugh at the poor black, white, brown, and yellow citizens of this great country? These citizens lack the opportunity to acquire a job to support their family. Is Mayor Bloomberg part of his fellow business associates and the national press that are involved in the biggest scam since the beginning of time? Our politicians and philanthropists should be doing everything they can to give our citizens an opportunity to obtain a job on an even playing field.

Mayor Bloomberg please become one of the true leaders in this country that want to crush the heartbreak of poverty, become a true leader that wants to take back our streets and reverse the course of criminal activity so that the future of our children are not in jeopardy. With unfair trade agreements on the rise our citizens can never become the masters of their fate. Mr. Bloomberg, we know you are a philanthropist, but this is not good enough. Release our children from the chains of discrimination and despair, release our children like you would a caged bird. **We need jobs with dignity!**

Athletes

To all sports figures in basketball, baseball, football, hockey, soccer, and golf with the prestige and power that you have earned, giving back to your community and country is a must. We are not soliciting money, just your endorsement of an opportunity for middle-class workers to have a job earning a livable wage. Many of our sports heroes came from poor communities themselves. We want to change this cycle of poverty and living in dangerous communities. Our children deserve better. There are millions of children that have never see a ballgame or gone to a sporting event because their parents are either unemployed, underemployed, or are part of Mitt Romney's 47% percent on government assistance. Being in this situation doesn't leave much money for sporting events. Seeing all the undesirable environments that many of these children face each day, should be enough to inspire our sports heroes to speak out for the lost middle-class. The parents of these children need jobs. Many of our sports heroes are African-American. Think back to how many of your friends were raised by a single parent, mainly the mother. Did you ever wonder why this revolving door is so hard to escape. There are certain inborn traits that come with being a man and one of them is the instinct and desire to take care of their family and be one of the breadwinners of the household. Having a job that gives a person the opportunity to support his family with dignity is the desire of each man. The warm feeling that comes over a man when one of his children says with pride "that's my dad" many African-American men learn at a young age that obtaining a job is a difficult task. Lacking a job leads to crime, drugs, abandoned families, and giving up at a young age with an"I- don't- care" and"you- have- to- die- sometime"attitude. Having your future mapped out at an early age makes it difficult to change this cycle of poverty and crime. Dropping out of high school seems to be a common practice in poverty and high crime areas. The people that do graduate from high school, where do they go from here? Lack of money and peer pressure makes college almost unattainable. Some do break free from this cycle and obtain a college degree and move on to greener pastures but a high percentage remain without employment and on government assistance. Many people say the only way to change this cycle is through education. This has been a common theme from educators over the past 60 years. This has helped many students breakaway from the cycle of poverty, but the percentages are very low. The easiest way a family can break the chains of poverty is having the opportunity to secure a job paying a living wage. Their children can learn and be proud of their parents and move on to the next step, higher education.

We must have jobs!

Many of these children live in areas where the best job is selling drugs and their homes are barely livable. This has to change. The majority of the parents want a better life for their children, but because of the out-sourcing of American jobs and the destruction of manufacturing com-munities throughout the United States these goals are not attainable. The multinational business executives claims the slaves in foreign countries will eventually become consumers. History has taught us different. When foreign employees of these unfair businesses request a raise or demand a living wage, the executives of these business threatens to or just moves their plants to another third world country. These employees will never become legitimate middle-class consumers. There are billions of people in third world countries that need and want employment. Unscrupulous business executives take advantage of their desire to obtain a better life.

Drive by shootings must stop now.we need jobs

Many of these executives claim outsourcing American jobs to foreign countries will benefit the United States. **This is the biggest scam since the beginning of time!** Meanwhile the United States needs jobs for people of all walks of life- rich or poor, college-educated or high school educated. We need jobs. Having a respectable job gives you the ability to buy a home, car, and raise a family in a safe environment.

All parents deserve an opportunity to live with dignity and raise their families with pride. You know yourselves being able to provide for your family and having a decent job does give one a feeling of self-worth. It is very difficult for most Americans to understand how business executives can complain about government entitlements. Part of the government assistance programs consist of unemployment benefits that are used by workers whose jobs have been outsourced.

There is a sore spot that the un-American executives would like to alter or eliminate and that's Medicare and Social Security benefits. These executives have already thrown the middle-class manufacturing worker under the bus. Now they would like to put enough tire tracks on them until they resemble the asphalt. Knowing the United States is suffering doesn't seem to concern the un-American big business executives and their board members. Seeing the red white and blue flying in the wind while our national anthem rings out means nothing to these un-American business executives and the unethical news reporters. Their heart and soul remains true to the American Benjamin's. If achieving more unethical riches means stepping on the middle-class manufacturing worker and forcing his head into the sand until he is no more, so be it. Being in bed with the un-American TV news organizations is going to assure them a positive report. The news media has brainwashed the American middle-class by saying this is the global economy at work, and it's good for America, **bullshit!**

The majority of African-Americans and the poor are still considered by big business and the unscrupulous news reporter as second class citizens. The un-American international business community and the unscrupulous news reporters laugh at African-Americans. They make fun of Martin Luther King. While in public many CEOs (new Masters of slaves) of big business continually express their desires to create jobs in the United States. If you want to work for slave wages, you have a job. Privately they express their thoughts by saying: anyone that is stupid enough to believe outsourcing jobs at slave labor wages is good for the United States, they deserved to be laughed at.

We come first!

If the press was truly honest they would go to the executives of big business and ask: what wages should American workers be paid so jobs can return to the United States. First this is never going to happen because the press is in bed with big business. If a miracle happened and the press approached big business with that question a straight answer would not be forthcoming. Laughter coming from big business and the national press toward the unemployed African-Americans whites Americans, and Hispanic would be deafening. Martin Luther King's speech "I have a dream" helped to change many laws that discriminated against African-Americans. The so-called Jim Crow laws were struck down. This helped eliminate separate drinking fountains, separate seating areas, separate schools, along with many other segregation laws. Many of the executives and board member of big business are just plain racist, their vision of an African American is paddling his way back to Africa. Martin Luther King's dream is turning into a nightmare. **Where are the jobs!** To cut entitlements without the opportunity to obtain a job is unconscionable. So we are asking sports figures to speak out for the common man and don't forget the friends and acquaintances you left behind.

The label that the national news networks has put on the backs of our African-American men is reprehensible. The news networks described the African-American man as lazy, high on drugs, future criminal, while deserting their families. Travel into any middle-class African-American community and you will notice the African-American men participating in all phases of their children's lives and being one of the breadwinners of the family maybe even sharing that honor with a spouse.

An African-American man living with his family in a middle-class setting is not lazy, is not high on drugs, and doesn't desert his family. The difference between men living in a middle-class environment and men living in the ghetto or poverty areas riddled with crime is a **Job**!

It is cheaper to provide an opportunity to obtain a job than being part of Mitt Romney's 47% percent on government assistance. The greedy un-American international business community is sucking the life out of our country. They must be denied. We must reverse course to give middle-class manufacturing workers a chance to thrive again.

We have made our case for middle class Americans to have a level playing field when it comes to jobs. Perhaps some governors, mayors, athletes, businesspeople, or TV and movie personalities have what it takes to stand up and let your voices be heard. In every generation there are special people who are willing to step up and take a chance. Are you going to be that one voice that helps turn the tide for the American middle class.

We come first!

Definition of a man

(1) Being one of the breadwinners in a family
(2) Just being one of the guys at the shop or place of employment
(3) That person who stands tall as he walks into the bank to cash his paycheck
(4) When one of his children looks up at him and asked, may I have a ball glove or doll and in your pocket is the money to make that request come true
(5) When vacation time comes around a trip to a theme Park or ocean is within reach
(6) When one of his children asked if a friend can come over and spend the night, he glances up at his home with pride and responds "any time"
(7) To accomplish the middle-class values so you can be a role model for your children to accomplish these goals a man needs a **job job job job job job job**

The so-called experts constantly talk about what it takes to turn this cycle of poverty and violence around. The answer is very easy **jobs**.

Whether you are black, white, brown, yellow, or red there is no better feeling than having a job and contributing to your family along with your children being proud of you.

We need action now! Jobs

Ellen

If you would like a breath of fresh air along with a ray of sunshine brought into your home each day reach for the remote and go to the channel that carries The Ellen Degeneres Show. Ellen is just one of those entertainers that can change a bad day into a good day. Having fun seems to be the main theme of her show. She starts off with music that turns your body into a rhythm machine. She proceeds into doing a dance up, down, and through the aisles of her audience. The smiles and laughter heard from her audience indicates that everyone is there for a good time. Whatever problems or pressures her audience has is to be left at the door, it's time to laugh and smile and let your problems flowed away. Ellen has that glimmer in her smile that seems to flow to her audience. The special guests that makes an appearance on her show always seem to enjoy the experience and the lightheartedness of her pleasant personality. Ellen's generosity and charitable efforts is well known throughout the celebrity community. Ellen has always been a giving and caring person. To achieve her celebrity status, hard work and determination is part of her character. Watching her TV show is a very popular and fun thing to do and that's why many people travel to her show just to sit in the audience and watch her entertaining juices flow.

At this time our country is in need of support for the forgotten middle-class. Even though Ellen is a very kind and charitable person, right now there are millions of people that are not looking for a handout but for a job. These future taxpaying citizens do not want to become part of **Mitt Romney's 47%** percent receiving government assistance. They need that one voice hoping it will echo into tens of millions of voices supporting the repeal of NAFTA and the unfair trade agreements.

It doesn't take a brain surgeon to see what CNN and the biased national news organizations along with the un-American executives of big business have done to this great country. The destruction of this country by the banks and their greedy employees has long past, the banks are fully funded and able to make loans. Millions and millions of jobs have been outsourced to slave labor countries in the past few years. **Outsourcing American jobs is absolutely the only reason for our high unemployment remaining at 7% percent along with millions more of underemployed citizens.**

With the support of NAFTA and unfair agreements the rich un-American international CEOs of big business, along with CNN and the national news organizations **(American job destroyers)** have caused

(1)   The overcrowding of our prisons.

(2)   The wage destruction of our manufacturing work force.

(3)   high unemployment.

(4)   Millions of American citizens that are underemployed.

(5)   Many districts where teachers have been laid off, there pay has been cut or is in jeopardy of being lowered.

(6)   The loss of trillions of dollars to our US treasury.

(7)   State and city workers paychecks and retirement checks being reduced.

(8)   Printing money to support the rich un-American international CEOs businesses.

(9)   Many communities due to layoffs and pay reduction lack a properly staff police force.

(10) Homes catching fire and burning to the ground along with the loss of children and adult lives, all because the un-American greedy rich would rather stuff their pockets full of

middle-class money leaving many communities with under-staffed fire departments and underpaid firefighters.

(11) Shoplifting is on the rise. In one community two young boys were arrested for shoplifting socks. The bankers in this country stole trillions of US dollars and to my knowledge not one went to jail. But steal a pair of socks and you get arrested and labeled as a juvenile delinquent. **Has the American public lost their mind?**

(12) Many children are going to experience a very sad Christmas. How does the greedy rich un-American CEOs of business and the biased national press, expect many segments of our country to experience a Merry Christmas.

(13) The brainwashing of the citizens in the US by the un-American press into thinking, sending American manufacturing jobs to slave labor countries is good for the United States.

(14) The catch phrase "global economy" to be accepted as an economy that the United States can compete.

(15) Much more harm to the American public than we have discussed.

Ellen if you have a heart will you lend your voice to the huddled masses that are having their future stolen by the un-American business executives along with the support of the American news media **(American job destroyers).**

(1) They are stealing middle-class's Medicare and retirement benefits. With the lack of revenue coming into the treasury cuts in benefits are eventually going to take place.

(2) They are stealing money from middle-class's paychecks. Too many people seeking too few jobs allow businesses to pay employees less.

(3) The catch phrase (global economy) is the name of the biggest scam perpetuated on the American public since the beginning of time.

(4) They are stealing many children's childhood and happiness. A family where the parents are unemployed or underemployed brings sadness and poverty to many households.

(5) We have self-serving idiots saying that the United States has the right to print money. Every citizen that pays taxes is subsidizing the un-American greedy rich's overseas businesses. This is how gullible the American public has become according to the greedy rich un-American CEOs of business.

War!

Securing a safe and prosperous future sometimes comes at a cost. At different times our US government has asked our citizens to take up arms against tyranny and criminal action by foreign governments. In doing so many of our soldiers gave up their lives so freedom, prosperity, and democracy in this country can remain strong. **Freedom doesn't come cheap**! World War I and World War II were not popular wars but they were necessary. During these wars many of our soldiers paid the ultimate price. The unfulfilled dreams, destroyed families, inhumane conditions, and much more contributed to lonely and broken hearts of many of our soldiers and their families

Then we had the Vietnam and Iraq wars. Both became very unpopular wars that were totally unnecessary. That didn't stop our arrogant and uncaring government from continually sending our troops overseas to lose arms, loose legs, return paralyze, some paid the ultimate price with their lives. Many of the uncaring government employees, who felt the need for another useless war had children of military age. Some had boys and some had as many as two girls who became of military age. When these government politicians were beating their chest for the annihilation of the citizens and governments of foreign countries they forgot that women were welcome in the military to serve their country with honor and dignity. Many of the war hungry politicians felt their children are more important than the average middle-class families' children.

PART I: WAR!

If a vote for war by a politician included a caveat that their children had to join the military service I'm sure more soul-searching would take place. If that caveat remained intact I'm sure many American soldiers lives, arms, legs, and much more would be spared because unnecessary wars would not take place.

Many of the international business executives that have little respect for our manufacturing community also have little respect for our men and women in the military service. Even though on the surface these businesspeople expressed thanks for a job well done. Underneath the surface they laugh and ridicule our men and women in uniform. These businesspeople know when our service personnel return from the rigors of war, obtaining a job with a future is less likely to happen. If our returning soldiers are fortunate enough to obtain employment it is more likely their pay will be quite a bit less for that same job just a few years ago. Underpaid American service personnel is caused by the outsourcing of American manufacturing jobs which creates a glut of un-employed workers. Too many people seeking too few jobs have caused the collapse of the wage structure of our American manufacturing work-ers. These un-American international businesspeople, who are the priv-ileged few that feel raping America is their right. Without having the national news media **(American job destroyers)** in their back pockets this would be an impossible task. The national news media profess to report on the economy in a balanced way so the citizens of the United States can have an opportunity to form their own opinions.

We come first!

By the un-American biased press eliminating all the facts pertaining to employment and our economy, it's difficult for the citizens of the United States to form an unbiased opinion.

The unethical journalists and press that plague our society fails to properly inform the public.

(1)   The biased press fails to inform the public how much money the slaves of foreign countries are paid for doing American jobs.

We need fact checkers!

(2)   When reporting on job creation at the end of each month and with zero to little growth in manufacturing and not explaining why this is taking place is unconscionable. There is only one reason and that's the outsourcing of manufacturing jobs to slave labor countries which the biased press fails to inform their listeners.

We need fact checkers!

(3)   The biased press fails to explain how the global economy works. The only way the American manufacturing workers

can compete is working for $.50 to $2.50 an hour. The global economy is the biggest scam played on the American public since the beginning of time.

We need fact checkers!

(4)   When the biased press reports on the national debt and how it's expanding by the minute, hour, day, and year, but doesn't report the numbers of manufacturing jobs lost to third world countries.

Our country has greedy rich un-American business executives that feel our government has the right to print money. This printing of money is subsidizing the outsourcing of American manufacturing jobs. The outsourcing of jobs has created a void in the collection of revenue for our treasury. Our government is printing money to fill that void and that's the same thing as subsidizing the outsourcing of American manufacturing jobs. Repealing NAFTA and unfair trade agreements along with effective use of tariffs is the only way to bring our country back to full prosperity again.

(5)   If our press can report on different civil wars, why do they refuse to show the expansion in Mexico and other foreign countries of buildings that are going to house American manufacturing worker's jobs. This is your un-American press at work.

We need fact checkers!

(6)   Having an honest and balanced press that represents all layers of our society, not just the rich is a must.

Our returning soldiers must have an opportunity to fulfill their dreams of going to college or obtaining a job with a future.

National Politicians

The future of 20 to 30 million unemployed and underemployed manufacturing workers are in the hands of our uninformed and misguided national politicians. These are the same group of people that depend on the un-American international business executives for their political lives. Our congressmen and congresswomen need to accept **"bribes"** in the form of donations to ensure their political future. The hatred of our congressional members by the public is understandable. The national debt crisis is continually mounting by the day, week, month, and year. Along with the lack of manufacturing jobs for the forgotten middle-class are in the hands and hearts of our representatives.

Most of our Congressional civil servants came into the political arena as idealists and statesmen wanting to create an atmosphere of goodwill and improving mankind. They were trying to make an honest contribution to society.

Starting out as local public servants, many were successful in improving their local communities giving them the confidence and desire to move on to a larger stage. It doesn't take long before all civil servants realize that representing your local district or state comes with a price. Our congressmen and congress women eventually become the puppets of the money people, whether the string pullers are local industrialists or executives that reside in un-American international business communities. Being the puppets of the money people was not there original goal. To ensure their reelection each politician must stand by their party and bow down to big business. Being a statesman and having a mind of your own in this political atmosphere is almost impossible.

Big business hires lobbyists to influence decisions made by our Congressional officials. Most lobbyists are able to meet with government officials or a staff member to present their side of certain issues. After the discussion of the lobbyists concerns are over, if money is not pledge to the congressperson's campaign that issue will fall by the wayside. Our Congress men and women main job is to get reelected. Approximately 25% percent of the US federal budget is wasted on unnecessary projects such as the bridge to nowhere or the $4 billion in tax breaks allocated for the five largest un-American oil companies, British Petroleum, Chevron, Conoco Phillips, Exxon Mobil, and Shell Oil. These five oil companies profits amount to approximately $120 billion a year. Eliminating the $4 billion in the yearly tax breaks for big oil and applying the money to elect our Senators and House Members while eliminating all unethical public and private political donations would easily create an atmosphere for fair and honest elections. The majority of our government officials, whether they be Democrat or Republican just want to do a good honest job. The problem is politics gets in the way.

The way the citizens of the United States elect their congressmen and congress women must change. We must bring some sanity and honest objectivity to the honorable position they hold. The citizens of the United States must become lobbyists. This is the only way sanity can return to the halls of Congress. To achieve that goal our government must set aside approximately $2-$4 billion for the election of our senators and House members each election year. **Outlawing all public and private donations is a must.** This would eliminate unfair elections by the rich puppet masters while creating a climate for statesman and honest public officials to reappear.

We look at the actions of our Congress with discussed and contempt. Imagine how the outside world views our Congressional leaders. We must change how we elect our congressmen and congresswomen.

Outlawing all public and private donations for our Congressional representatives is a must and our citizens well receive $500 billion in savings each year!

We elect our House of Representatives and Senators to represent the people that elected them. After being elected it seems that the **"party"** whether it be Democrat or Republican, becomes more important than their constituents.

Outlawing all public and private donations for our Congressional representatives is a must and the United States would receive $500 Billion windfall in savings each year!

With our national news commentators being in the back pockets of the un-American international business executives, the chances of my proposal being discussed is slim to none. My proposal of setting aside $2-$4 billion each election year for congressional elections will never see the light of day.

Outlawing all public and private donations for our Congressional leaders' election will ensure honest and fair elections. Having politicians that are not in the back pockets of big business and the rich will create a savings of approximately $500 billion each year for the citizens of the United States.

Final solution!

The real Dracula was born in 1431 in Transylvania he didn't sleep in coffins or suck blood. He became a prince and was noted for his brutality. Not having modern equipment, Dracula's famous method of eliminating undesirable people was to have them impaled. The only problem the un-American international businesspeople and the national news organizations **(American job destroyers)** have with impaling 25 million people is, it would take up too much land.

Hitler used the oven method.

The South lynching was their choice for elimination.

Slave traders used the chain method, shackle a group together then throw the chain overboard.

These are extreme unrealistic methods to cure the unemployment and underemployment crisis in the United States. The average middle-class person does not want to be a burden on society. Their main goal is to have the opportunity to secure a job on a level playing field, nothing more just an equal chance to have a middle-class life in the United States.

We come first!

Sending jobs to a foreign country paying slave labor wages eliminates a large segment of our society from achieving those middle-class goals. The policies of the rich businesspeople must change along with the national news organizations **becoming a voice of all the people not just the rich. There is no such thing as a global economy that benefits the United States. NAFTA and unfair trade agreements must be repealed along with using effective tariffs.**

We come first!

PART II

Introduction to Part II

Delphi's push to move jobs to slave labor countries created approximately 75,000 jobs in Mexico. Management felt the unions demand for a fair and living wage was excessive. The true reason was cheap slave labor.

I expose the unethical employees in management that mishandled millions and millions of dollars of retiree's and stockholders' money. Vanguard witnessed firsthand the unethical decisions made by management. If this trend was companywide it's obvious that this behavior contributed to the downfall of Delphi.

Opening to Part II

My apprenticeship as a tool and die maker was served at an eight-man shop in Canfield, Ohio called "Demes Tool and Die. In the 1960's receiving a tool and die apprenticeship was the equivalent to a college education. Participation in a tool and die apprenticeship required four years of on-the-job training as well as attending night classes related to the trade. Demes Tool and Die created the opportunity for me to receive an apprenticeship and that greatly influenced my decision to offer apprenticeships when I started my company, Vanguard Die and Machine.

While working toward my journeyman's card at Demes Tool and Die, I was fortunate to have journeyman die makers that were excellent teachers and quite knowledgeable about the trade. Through the years, most of the journeyman die makers with whom I served my apprenticeship passed away, but my mind still drifts back to my apprenticeship days and the memories are still fresh. Their knowledge and skill laid the foundation for my advancement in the tool and die trade.

During my years as an apprentice I became friends with a designer and another apprentice die maker. As our friendship grew, our conversation turned to starting our own tool and die shop. After becoming a journeyman die maker my desire to have my own shop grew stronger. Finally, there was an agreement that the three of us would join forces to start a tool and die shop. Everyone was well qualified with great work ethics and drive needed to succeed. Initially it looked like success was in the future for our partnership.

My initial evaluation of the future of our business was wrong. Having partners with strong personalities was a very difficult challenge for the three of us. The company was in peril very soon after the start up, because the three of us could not work out our differences. After a difficult eight months, the three of us decided to go our separate ways and the company was dissolved. This experience with business partners was important as well as the unfortunate outcome of our alliance. This would influence my decision years later about taking on a partner in my future business.

General Motors at Lordstown, Ohio and Packard Electric in Warren, Ohio were the largest manufacturing corporations in the local area. These companies had not started hiring many journeyman die makers or machinist when I started in the trades. When Lordstown and Packard started to hire journeyman machinist and die makers it caused many problems with the local small shops.

After losing their skilled help to Packard and Lordstown many shops had to close their doors. The shops that remained opened only offered machine operator status instead of a journeyman card. By not offering apprenticeships the local shops could avoid losing their employees to larger shops. I was one of the people that left the shop where I received my training and was hired in at Packard Electric as a tool and die maker. This took place not long after my first venture into owning a business with partners was dissolved.

I did have the foresight to purchase the machinery from our bankrupt company. Some of the machinery was placed in storage and the balance was moved into my garage. Having machinery operating in my garage made picking up small jobs easy. As I was closing in on the age of thirty eight, my children were growing up and going off to college. The desire to own my own shop resurfaced. Being a newspaper carrier from the age of 12 to 18 could of had an influence on my wanting to have my own business. For six years I was a newspaper carrier seven days a week, rain or shine, I delivered the local newspaper. Hard work was always in my life and my entrepreneurial spirit was kicking into gear. Vanguard Die and Machine Incorporated was born on March 1984.

Having our employees receive quality training was first and foremost in our minds, this helped guarantee the success of our company. We received applicants from the local trade schools and through advertisements in the local newspaper. After the interview process was completed and the hiring of employees was put in motion Vanguard Die and Machine's doors were open. While working at Demes Tool and Die, I was one of those employees that enjoyed their job. Maybe that was one reason why I excelled at my trade.

Without an apprenticeship and a journeyman's card, it is very difficult to get hired by a large company. Lacking a journeyman's card, there must be proof of eight years experience of on the job training. This can be very difficult to prove because you must go back to each shop where you were employed and request from the owner or Foreman the documentation showing what machines you had operated and the amount of time spent on each machine. The shop owners were reluctant to give that information out. The shop owners were unhappy with the amount of time and money spent on training an employee (which is considerable) and now he would prefer to work for a larger company. Since few shops were cooperative, the best alternative was to get an apprenticeship. One of Vanguard's goals was to make sure each employee had the opportunity to receive an apprenticeship if they so desired. After working for a period of time each employee was offered the opportunity to be placed on the apprenticeship program.

The apprenticeship program was managed by the state of Ohio and each apprentice would be required to register with the state. It was Vanguard's job to monitor the apprentices to ensure they followed state guidelines. One of the main goals of Vanguard was to maintain a very high level of training for our apprentices. Most of the apprentices that obtained their journeyman's card from Vanguard Die and Machine were either hired by Packard Electric in Warren, Ohio or the General Motors Lordstown plant. Vanguard eventually became a very important supplier of dies, assemblies, and spare parts for Packard

Electric. Hiring a journeyman from Vanguard, Packard Electric knew they were hiring an employee that was quite knowledgeable about the type of tooling that needed to be produced. During this period of time it was almost impossible to receive a tool and die apprenticeship from a local job shop.

The main reason why this was the case is that when a die or machine shop puts an employee on an apprenticeship program the apprentice is to operate each type of machine if work is available for that particular machine. The apprentice also receives instructions on how to assemble, try out, and debug a die. This process is very expensive, because the training is usually handled by a journeyman who is one of the highest-paid employees in the shop. This translates to the highest-paid employee serving as an instructor on how to operate a machine efficiently and safely. After the apprentice receives instructions on the operation of the machine he must be monitored for quality and safety. Again this process is usually handled by a journeyman. It takes between six months to two years before an apprentice is able to increase his skill level on each machine. During the four-year apprenticeship program there are quite a few machines where this process is repeated. When the salaries of the journeyman and apprentice are added together, the cost of a project goes up considerably and, most of the time, very little is being accomplished.

Even though offering apprenticeships is a very expensive direction to take, this was the decision made early on at Vanguard. We could have easily trained machine operators, which is a much cheaper route to take. Having machine operators also creates a more stable work force because a company can limit a person's skill level which makes an employee less likely to move on to a new employer. A machine operator's pay scale is also much lower than a journeyman's. Vanguard Die and Machine could easily have increased our earnings by going the way of training machine operators and not offering apprenticeships. Being the son of a steelworker, I felt lucky to have accomplished what I had, and giving back a little to society wasn't going to kill me. This was the direction we chose.

Most machinists and die makers who start their own business are very knowledgeable at their trade. Becoming very proficient at your trade does not, however, guarantee success. Having the traits of a work-aholic also comes into play, because the hours can be very long and hard in the beginning. Having those two attributes in hand, the next step is to develop a sense of business. Learning to deal with suppliers, custom-ers, money, employees, are just part of the challenges that help develop a successful business. The unwritten rule is if you last five years, the success of being a small business owner seems to be assured. Not being able to handle the day to day struggles and pressures of business can contribute to an early closing.

The direction that Vanguard Die and Machine took was to design and build stamping dies and also machining general parts. Our first cus-tomer is still located on the West side of Cleveland. The first purchase order from him was receive in 1984, and the last purchase order from that company was finished in 2012. Through the ups and downs of busi-ness it was a twenty-eight year adventure. Our customer base was al-ways growing, and maintaining good relationships was a priority. When you understand your customer's needs, and they understand what capa-bilities your shop brings to the table, a strong and lasting relationship starts to take shape.

As Vanguard was developing a clientele in the stamping and ma-chining industry, we received our first request from Packard Electric. As it turned out, Packard was looking for a local shop to turn around quick jobs and wanted to know if Vanguard had any interest in developing a long-term relationship. We acknowledged our interest and were looking forward to the opportunity of doing business with them. Vanguard Die and Machine was a very quality oriented shop, so our relationship with Packard Electric advanced very quickly. We went from a few hundred thousand dollars in sales to almost 2,000,000 in a short period of time. In the beginning the relationship between Vanguard and Packard was based on trust, loyalty to our customer, and a positive outlook. Packard electric receive on time delivery of quality parts and assemblies at a very fair and competitive price. This working relationship lasted twenty-eight years, but the last 12 were marred by the customer's show of favoritism to a certain vendor. Ineffective management in those years costs Delphi(they changed from Packard to Delphi by that time) millions upon millions of dollars in overpayments to preferred vendors. Working through the 80s, 90s, and part of the 21st century without any complaints or distractions from the customer was a credit to our work force. A small company lives and dies by its the guidelines set up by management.

From the time our shop opened until it's closing, technology altered how the tool and die and machining industry operated. In the early years, a die maker would be given prints to a die, he would then operate different machines to manufacture each detail. Heat treating each detail was the next operation, followed by grinding, assembling, try out, and debugging the dies. Using a surface grinder, a die maker created angles, radii, and many other shapes to precision dimensions. This was a common method used for the last hundred years. The introduction of wire electrical discharge machines (wire EDM had the capability of machining any radius is, angles, and other shapes to within 1/10000 of an inch. This eliminated the cost of grinding shapes, angles, and radii by the die maker. To keep up with and obtain the rapid changes in technology, Vanguard purchased seven wire EDM machines. Some of these machines came at a cost of several hundred thousand dollars. Our next step was to become familiar with CNC machining centers. Our original thought was to purchase two but demands for our services from Packard electric for more precision details, assemblies and dies, convinced Vanguard that more machines were required. Vanguard eventually purchased seven machining centers to accommodate the orders from Packard Electric. Through the years many machines were sold and replaced that were newer and equipped with more modern technology. This continued the process and philosophy of Vanguard's management: quality machinery helps the employees manufacture quality parts and assemblies.

The initial request for quotes originated in the make die area at Packard Electric. This area housed high precision dies and our job was the support of these dies. Our original support consisted of manufacturing interchangeable high precision parts. These parts usually had a tolerance of plus or minus 1/10000.

Over the next 18 years the purchasing personnel at Packard changed about every year or two. These frequent changes with purchasing agents in the make die area work in Vanguard's favor. Not having the same buyer or expediter for any length of time gave Vanguard the chance to grow. Buyers with a short lifespan made it difficult to develop a close personal relationship with the suppliers. Packard had a preferred list of suppliers that had established a reputation for doing quality work and Vanguard was on that list. Being on the preferred bidders list gave Vanguard the opportunity to receive most quotes coming out of the make die area.

The next step was pricing, if Vanguard could produce quality parts at a competitive cost our growth at Packard was assured.

After developing an hourly rate, which consists of labor and over-head(heat treat, electricity, holiday pay, health insurance, rent, and office support) material and delivery costs were built into each quote. Material and delivery costs could fluctuate so they were added to the quote separately. Packard had two types of quoting: spot buys and blanket orders. A spot buy is when Packard issues a list of items to quote with a specific date for delivery. The supplier attached a price to these parts of various quantities and returned them back to Packard. Packard's delivery requirements were approximately 30 days. With delivery being standard the low bidder usually received the purchase order for the quoted parts.

To be eligible for the opportunity to quote blanket orders a supplier had to have completed the Targets for Excellent Program. Packard had initiated the program to ensure that each supplier understood what requirements were expected. The supplier had to develop a company manual outlining everything from processing the material to final inspection.

Processing material: after the material is received in the shop, each machine and employee involved in the manufacturing of parts from this material is documented.

Final inspection: each detail is inspected along with documentation showing that 100% percent of the part was inspected. Any employee that was involved in the machining process did not participate in the inspection process. Inspection sheets were signed by the inspector, dated, and a copy was attached to the print. Vanguard maintained inspection forms for all the parts manufactured at Vanguard. In the beginning Packard periodically checked our inspection sheets for accuracy; this procedure was very short-lived. The inspection documents were to be made available to Packard upon request for approximately two years. If need be Packard could place a call to Vanguard inquiring about the status of their orders. Having this procedure in place did help Vanguard track Packard's parts and, when needed, we were able to expedite critical parts for early delivery.

Our Targets for Excellence manual was developed over a year's time and was approved in intervals, by different teams from Packard. Completing the Targets for Excellence program allowed Vanguard to be added to the preferred bidders list of suppliers. We were now qualified to bid on blanket orders.

After qualifying for the preferred bidders list, a supplier would receive a list of parts to quote. Prints would be provided by Packard along with the approximate volume of parts that would be needed each month as a guideline for a supplier to control his inventory. The cost would be established considering the cost of manufacturing each detail along with the cost of maintaining an inventory.

After establishing a cost for the quote it would be sent back to Packard. Packard would review the prices for each detail, take the lowest price submitted, and reduce the cost between 2 and 5 percent. The quote would be resubmitted back to the Packard for reevaluation. These were called target prices. Each supplier would be asked if they could meet the target price. If more than one supplier met the target price, Packard would go additional rounds in the bidding process until one supplier was left. That supplier would be awarded the blanket contract for those details, lasting between one to two years. A blanket contract meant, for the duration of the contract, Packard was to buy the parts or assemblies from that supplier. Packard expected a thirty- day delivery and it was the supplier's job to maintain an inventory to meet Packard's request for parts. The relationship between Packard and Vanguard in the make die area lasted from 1984 to 2002. During those 18 years in the make die area Vanguard never encountered one quality issue. We manufactured at least 3000 different details with the yearly volume of each part fluctuating. Some years orders had a volume of between four to several hundred pieces for each detail.

When the year 1995 rolled around Packard Electric decided it need-ed a name change. Their new handle was going to be Delphi Automotive Systems.

Even though there was a name change the personnel and ideology remained the same. Another major change took place at Delphi in the 1990s. In may of 1999, Delphi's spinoff from General Motors was com-pleted, making Delphi an independent company.

By the time 2002 rolled around, Vanguard was one of the top three suppliers, making thousands upon thousands of parts for Packard in the make die area.

Starting around the year 2002, Delphi decided it no longer wanted to have control of the purchasing department that handled spare parts and assemblies in the make die area. This new department was going to oversee the details and assemblies that Vanguard was supplying to Delphi. Outsourcing the purchasing of this type of work was supposed to save Delphi money. Instead through the years, it has potentially cost Delphi $75-$100 million dollars. The company chosen to han-dle Delphi's purchasing was located in Atlanta, Georgia and went by the name of Vanguard Distributors. Not being close to upper management, we never knew what decision process they used to justify outsourcing the purchasing of certain manufactured products. What I do know is that standard Delphi policy was that a person in upper management who resigned from Delphi agreed not to take a job with a Delphi vendor for at least two years. This was confirmed at a meeting with Delphi's law Department investigator, Jerry. George Boardwalk was an employee in management at Delphi who came under those guidelines. After resigning from Delphi, and before the two-year limit had passed, George Boardwalk turned up at Vanguard Distributors. The rumor was that George Boardwalk was given an exemption to the two-year rule. It would be interesting to know if George Boardwalk had anything to do with Vanguard Distributors receiving the outsourcing contract from Delphi.

At this time Vanguard Die and Machine has no direct knowledge that George Boardwalk was involved in the decision-making process that resulted in Vanguard Distributors being awarded the contract to take over the purchasing department for machine parts and assemblies.

Vanguard distributors, being located in Georgia, needed employees in the Warren, Ohio area. Bill Blasko, Larry Bolan, Cindy Silo, and Greg Smith were hired by Vanguard Distributors to head up the new department in Warren Ohio.

They also had two Delphi employees Dean Hansen and George Story assisting Vanguard Distributors. When Bill Blasco would refer to Vanguard Distributors he used the term "the team" so we will bow to Bill Blasco's wishes.

Under the new teams direction, to speed up delivery it was decided that thirty day delivery was not acceptable. Under the new teams guidelines each vendor was notified that a change in delivery was going to take place. The allotted time for delivery was going to be shortened to ten days. Each vendor was going to be given a certain number of parts that needed to be maintained in stock for each item. Vanguard Die and Machine had 2500 to 3000 parts on blankets at that time. That meant

Vanguard Die and Machine had to go to each detail we had on blankets and make extra parts to keep in stock to satisfy the ten day delivery requirements. Each vendor was given an update on delivery once a month.

Needless to say Vanguard had a monumental task ahead of them to satisfy the teams requirements. Making extra parts for thousands of items in a short period of time was going to be a very difficult task. Vanguard questioned Bill Blasko about shortening the delivery time by twenty days. His response was that we were the only shop questioning him concerning this change. We later found out that Bill Blasko's response was not true. This is not going to be the only time Bill Blasko's honesty is questioned The investigator from Delphi's legal Department, Jerry, also had some concerns.

Vanguard Die and Machine was having difficulty maintaining their normal customer base while being required to manufacture extra parts for a couple thousand details. Even though extra parts were being added to the inventory, payment was not forthcoming until an order was placed for that particular detail. Most of the orders that Vanguard received from the make die area consisted of high precision parts, plus or minus one $1/10,000$. When these parts were delivered they went from our shop to Delphi's inventory. Very seldom were these parts used sooner than three weeks to a month after delivery. Vanguard always made a partial delivery within the ten days allotted. The balance of the order was always shipped befor the old thirty day requirement. A meeting was requested by Bill Blasko to review our delivery problems. During that meeting Bill Blasko brought to our attention that it took Vanguard Die and Machine on average twenty- three days to get a completed order in-house at Delphi. Bill **Blasko** acknowledged that Vanguard always made a partial delivery within the ten days allotted. He also confirmed to me that Delphi never had any downtime on dies due to late deliveries. Bill Blasko stated to me that the usage of these parts did not start immediately and it took three to six weeks before a part was needed.

The fact that Delphi received a complete order from Vanguard Die and Machine with an average delivery date of twenty three -days indicated that Vanguard was thirteen days past due. Using the old delivery time of thirty days showed that Vanguard would have been one week early.

After Dean Hansen and Bill Blasko sabotaged Vanguard Die and Machine forcing Vanguard to withdraw from the make die area the 30 day delivery was reinstated.

As the meeting progressed Bill Blasko informed Vanguard that the team decided to resource about 800 of our details to other vendors because of our delivery problems. Not once during the meeting was a quality issue discuss. Until that time we serviced Delphi for eighteen years without one complaint about quality, pricing, or delivery. Vanguard was also going to be put on hold for future orders. This was to last three months. The details that were removed from our blankets were quality parts. These parts always had good volume and high reorder status. I guess if you were a vendor and friends with Bill Blasko and Dean Hansen, this was a happy day for you. This was not a happy day for Vanguard or Vanguard's employees because of Bill Blasko and Dean Hansen's favoritism policy, thireteen employees at Vanguard had to be terminated.

Some of the employees that were terminated were buying cars, homes, and raising a family. A family losing their health insurance was also a terrible blow.

Some of the employees that lost their jobs were in the middle of their apprenticeship. Losing your apprenticeship and job was a life altering experience. A job you can replace, but being accepted into another apprenticeship program was very difficult. My wife and I felt a deep sadness for these good employees but our hands were tied. This is not the last time that Bill Blasko and Dean Hansen caused havoc at our shop, for no reason other than favoritism towards other vendors. The sad part was after our parts were resourced to other vendors they also had difficulty with the ten day delivery and the team eventually moved the delivery back to thirty days. This was too late for Vanguard's laid-off employees.

Bill Blasko indicated that the 800 parts were to be returned to Vanguard if over a three-month period our delivery improved to at least 92% percent on time delivery. Vanguard Die and Machine improved its delivery to 96% percent to 100% percent for seven straight months. Instead of restoring the 800 details to Vanguard, Bill Blasko, Dean Hansen, Larry Bolan, and the rest of the team was going to make it much more difficult for Vanguard to operate in the make die area.

About seven months had passed since the meeting with Bill Blasko. This puts the time at late November or early December 2002. A luncheon was set up between Larry Bolan and myself, to take place at Enzo's Restaurant. Before the luncheon took place I went over the monthly reports that have been supplied to Vanguard by Bill Blasko and the team. The report showed that Vanguard had over the previous seven months maintain an average of 98% percent on-time delivery. Our prices must have been good because in other areas at Delphi, Vanguard was receiving 70% percent to 80% percent of work we quoted. Our quality never came into question. Vanguard was doing everything we could to meet all of the demands of Bill Blasko and the team.

The luncheon started off quite well, with Larry Bolan's praising of Vanguard. Larry Bolan stated that Vanguard was achieving all the goals that the team expected. The team that Bill Blasko continually referred to consisted of Vanguard distributor's employees and Delphi's employees. He went on to say that our delivery was excellent, our pricing was very good, and no other vendor had achieved better quality than Vanguard. Everything was going well, but having worked with Bill Blasko, Dean Hansen, Larry Bolan, and the team, I knew there was something in the wind to turn this luncheon on its ear.

The storm arrived when Larry Bolan suggested that people at Delphi thought Vanguard Distributors and Vanguard Die and Machine were the same company. To say there was a problem was baffling to me, since Vanguard Die and Machine had been doing work for the team for over a year, and this had never been brought to our attention until now. Vanguard has been supplying machine parts and assemblies for many areas throughout Delphi and this situation had never come to light. The Delphi Accounting Department seems to be able to tell the difference because Vanguard Die and Machine has never received Vanguard Distributors check by mistake.

I felt Larry Bolan hadn't completed his thought: since the team felt there was confusion between Vanguard Die and Machine and Vanguard Distributors something had to be done to remedy the situation. The teams remedy for the situation was that Vanguard Die and Machine had to join forces with another machine shop as a partner. I sat back in my chair in disbelief, it seemed like forever. At first I thought this was a joke, but Larry assured me this was no joke. My response to Larry Bolan was, this didn't make any sense. Our relationship with Delphi and the make die area had lasted eighteen years, and to place an unreasonable demand like this to Vanguard was quite baffling. Larry Bolan again stated that this was a must for Vanguard, to move forward. He again stated that Vanguard must take on a local machine shop as a partner. As the conversation progressed, Larry Bolan, for the third time, demanded that Vanguard take on a local machine shop as a partner for us to be able to move forward with the team.

Again I leaned back in my seat, as you can imagine I was quite upset about the demands being put on Vanguard by Larry Bolan and the team. The make die area was a major part of our business. After Larry Bolan made his demands, and knowing that I was quite upset he dangled the carrot. He stated that if Vanguard would take on a local machine shop as a partner the team would guarantee Vanguard 200 orders a month. The additional 200 orders a month could easily double the size of our company.

Larry then brought to my attention the fact that the team had complete control over Vanguard Die and Machine's destiny. His tone of voice indicated that we better take the offer or else. Larry stated that Vanguard's opportunity of receiving any new orders from Delphi was not going to happen, along with the possibility of being sabotage by the team. If this offer was not accepted the team was in the position to discredit Vanguard. We would no longer remain on the preferred bidders list in the make die area.

When this meeting was originally scheduled I thought it was to reinstate Vanguard. Instead it turned out to be a luncheon from hell. We had not received any new quotes from the team for the past eight months. Even though for the past seven months we had 98% on-time delivery, no quality issues, and for Vanguard to receive the number of details that we had on blankets our pricing had be very competitive. With the credentials that we have just discussed it was hard to believe that the team would sabotage Vanguard. Even though 800 details were purged from Vanguard's blankets we still controlled a large quantity of parts. These details were still on our blankets and to lose these parts it would be devastating to our business. I asked Larry if this was his idea and his response was:" I am just the messenger."

After having the ultimatum presented to Vanguard I was quite shaken up and was trying to regain my composure. We were discussing the future of a business that I had started from nothing.

The small success that I had achieved was in jeopardy. Knowing the pitfalls of having a partner in my first business venture, I knew taking on a partner was never going to happen. My proposal to Larry was that Vanguard would set up a separate company under a different name so we could process our parts through the new company. This would eliminate all confusion about the two Vanguards. After a couple moments of silence, Larry indicated to me that he did not have the authority to okay this proposal. He would have to take this proposal back to the team. Whatever their decision, he would make sure that Vanguard received an answer. To this day we have not received a phone call, fax, or e-mail from Larry Bolan or the team concerning our offer.

The luncheon from hell was over and I was left bewildered and stunned by Larry's proposal. After returning to the shop my first reaction was to call Bill Blasko and discuss with him what had transpired between Larry and me that day. My first call to Bill Blasko went unanswered, along with many calls after that. The telephone call between Bill

Blasko and myself was finally completed. I explained to Bill that during the luncheon with Larry, we had an unpleasant ultimatum presented to us. I told him Larry insisted that Vanguard Die and Machine take on a local machine shop as a partner in order to continue doing business in the make die area. If this did not happen the team would do everything in its power to force Vanguard off the preferred bidders list even if it took sabotaging Vanguard. Bill Blasko seemed a little uncomfortable with the direction the conversation was taking. His response was that Larry was going to be reprimanded for presenting that proposal to Vanguard or implying that the team would try to sabotage Vanguard or do us any harm. I pointed out to Bill that Larry was just the messenger and didn't have the power, or understanding of business, to come up with this on his own. Bill Blasko finally admitted that the team had a meeting and what Larry Bolan presented to Vanguard was the result of that meeting.

After admitting that everything Larry had presented to Vanguard was true, and confirming that Larry Bolan was instructed by the team to do so, Bill Blasko made a quick exit off the phone. With the major part of Vanguard's business being in the make die area, perhaps Bill Blasko and the team were thinking that Vanguard would consider, part of a business was better than no business at all. If we hadn't had a bad experience at our previous business venture, the thought of accepting their proposal of taking on a partner might have crossed our mind but it didn't happen.

We later learned that an employee in upper management at Delphi had a friend that started his own shop and was working out of his garage. The team was giving him the opportunity to do work for Delphi. At the first meeting that Vanguard Die and Machine had with Vanguard Distributors (the team) they indicated that one of their assignments was to eliminate shops that staff under twenty five employees, so for anyone to have a shop doing work for Delphi out of their garage seemed unusual.

Thinking back to the luncheon that Larry Bolan had with Vanguard, when he insisted that Vanguard take a local machine shop as a partner, one might wonder whether this was the shop that the team had in mind.

Even though Vanguard did not accept the proposal offered by the team, it seemed a little far-fetched that a large company like Delphi would stoop to sabotaging one of their vendors, but there were millions of dollars of business at stake.

In January 2002 Vanguard Die and Machine received its first Problem Reporting Resolution (PRR) on a major part. This meant that there was a problem with a part, and to identify the problem the part would be sent to an independent lab for inspection. An inspection report showing where the dimension problem exists would be sent to the vendor and Delphi. The vendor would report back to Delphi explaining what corrective action needed to take place to bring the part within tolerance. After the part came back from the lab, the inspection report indicated that everything was within tolerance. Not having an inspection report from the lab did not stop a team member from going to meetings with Delphi management and saying: that Vanguard Die and Machine had received a PRR and was having quality problems. When future meetings were held the team never informed management that Vanguard was not having quality issues because the inspection report indicated no corrective action was needed. By not informing management the truth about Vanguard, the people at the meeting came to believe that Vanguard was having quality issues. I had a friend who attended one of those meetings, and he informed me that a member from the team was complaining about Vanguard not having air conditioning and this was causing a quality issue. This was a total lie, because Vanguard did have air conditioning and we were not having quality issues. Thinking back to the meeting at which Larry Bolan had said, if Vanguard did not take on a partner, the team,(which consisted of Vanguard Distributor's employees and Delphi's employees) was going to sabotage Vanguard Die and Machine; as hard as it is to believe the sabotage had begun.

Vanguard tried to create a better environment between Bill Blasko and the team. Vanguard tried to contact Dean Hansen and Bill Blasko by e-mail, fax, and telephone, but as usual there wasn't any response from either person. Vanguard Die and Machine had been one of the largest suppliers of parts and assemblies for eighteen years to the make die area before the team came into play. Through the quoting system, we had accumulated thousands of details on our blankets, saving Delphi millions and millions of dollars. Having the respect of the past purchasing agents along with employees on the floor who receive our parts, knowing there was not going to be a quality issue, was not enough. It was obvious that the team was making every effort to distance themselves from Vanguard. Communication with the team became nonexistent.

With Dean Hansen, Bill Blasko, and the team avoiding all communication with Vanguard, another approach had to be explored. We have worked with many buyers throughout our eighteen- years relationship at Delphi. Our thoughts were to see if one of these buyers would assist Vanguard in communicating with Bill Blasko and Dean Hansen. We contacted Ed Thompson, who worked close to Bill Blasko's office. At this time Ed Thompson still used our services but very little work was generated from his area. Ed Thompson said he would assist Vanguard in trying to reestablish communication with the team. Direct communication wasn't to be, so whenever Vanguard wanted to contact Dean Hansen or Bill Blasko and expect an answer we first had to contact Ed Thompson. Dean Hansen and Bill Blasko were just a couple of assholes.

- Vanguard Die and Machine had served Delphi for eighteen years, manufacturing millions upon millions of dollars of work but all those years of dedicated honest service and saving Delphi millions of dollars meant nothing. We had to resort to a third-party for communication; this was just plane crazy. Help from Ed Thompson was greatly appreciate, because without him our communication with Bill Blasko and Dean Hansen would have been nonexistent. Vanguard offered to meet with Bill Blasko and Dean Hansen to work out our differences, but the olive branch was refused. No matter what Vanguard proposed, it was knocked down by Bill Blasko and the team.

After receiving a few more PRRs, and as usual the parts were sent to an independent lab and returned without any tolerance issues. This did not stop the team from going to meetings and giving negative reports on Vanguard. Having the team ignore the full truth and fail to explain to management that the PRRs were bogus and that the parts were within tolerance was highly unethical. Management was receiving reports concerning Vanguard that were absolute lies. At this time a decision had to be made whether to stay in the make die area and hope for the best or opt out of the program. You would think a company with eighteen years of experience in an area without any major complaints would be a preferred supplier. Before the team arrived, Vanguard Die and Machine saved Delphi millions of dollars through the years. The percentage of parts that Vanguard was low bid on usually ran about 70% percent so for the team to be able to place purchase orders with their favorite vendor's for a higher cost, it seems like Vanguard had to go.

Another reason why Vanguard did not get involved in taking on a partner as suggested by Larry Bolan, Bill Blasko, and Dean Hansen was because we were afraid there was going to be more involved than met the eye. Being promised by Larry Bolan and Bill Blasko 200 orders a month was very suspicious. Besides taking on a partner, we were concerned that our obligation to Dean Hansen and Bill Blasko may end up being much more than Vanguard bargained for. These concerns that we discussed at Vanguard, explain why we turned our backs on the deal with Blasko and Hansen.

It was in the early part of March 2003 that Vanguard decided to make one last push for acceptance from the team." We sent an e-mail to the team that all the PRR's were in compliance according to Atco metrology lab, so quality was not an issue. Our on-time delivery was never lower than 96% percent since July 2002, which indicated that our seven months of on-time delivery was well within the teams requirements. After eighteen years of honest and productive relationship with Delphi and meeting all requirements from the team, Vanguard was still denied quoting or spot by status. Multiple phone calls and requests to Dean Hansen, Bill Blasko, and Larry Bolan have been ignored regarding our position with Delphi. If our differences are unrepairable, Vanguard would have to opt out of the make die area."

The e-mail that Vanguard Die and Machine received from Bill Blasko stated that the team wanted an elite group of suppliers capable of achieving quality delivery and pricing goals. He further stated that decisions were necessary to reduce the number of suppliers based on these metrics and that it was difficult and unfortunate that during the process Vanguard Die and Machine had been unable to develop quickly enough to meet the goals. The teams own record showed that Vanguard had 96% percent on time delivery with no major quality issues, and our records indicate that we were receiving approximately 70% of details quoted. Vanguard met their metrics and surpassd them.

Every word from Bill Blasko was a total lie! Bill Blasko sending this e-mail showed the teams integrity was missing and honesty was not their policy. It also showed that Bill Blasko and the team were at the forefront of sabotaging Vanguard Die and Machine. The favoritism that was festering within Delphi over the years caused a loss of millions upon millions of dollars. As much as $75 to $100 million could have been lost over the years. Delphi claims it doesn't have the money to pay former employees health insurance or retirement benefits. It's easy to understand why Delphi went bankrupt if the other departments had the same style of management.

Delphi's law department finally got involved and did some investigating. Vanguard was asked to submit some e-mails we receive from Delphi management. We submitted the e-mail that Bill Blasko had sent to Vanguard along with the teams records on Vanguard's delivery and quality. This showed that Bill Blasko and Dean Hansen sabotaged Vanguard Die and Machine. The law departments involvement didn't surface until many years later.

Month	vendor's name	status	delivery	major/PRR
July 02	Vanguard Die and Machine SB hold		96%	0
Aug 02	Vanguard Die and Machine SB hold		98%	0
Sep 02	Vanguard Die and Machine SB hold		100%	0
Oct 02	Vanguard Die and Machine SB hold		100%	0
Nov 02	Vanguard Die and Machine SB hold		98%	0
Dec02	Vanguard Die and Machine SB hold		100%	0
Jan 03	Vanguard Die and Machine SB hold		100%	1
Feb 03	Vanguard Die and Machine SB hold		97%	0

This is a partial graph that Vanguard Die and Machine received from Bill Blasko and the team outlining Vanguard's progress each month. As you can see the name of the company proceeds the list of Vanguard's accomplishments.

(1) SB HOLD: Vanguard die and machine was denied the opportunity to quote new work because of late deliveries. As you can see that was a lie.

(2) DELIVERIES: Vanguard's on time deliveries would be the envy of most businesses. In the meeting that Vanguard had with Larry Bolan a couple months earlier he relayed to Vanguard that our delivery was excellent.

(3) MAJOR PRR: Problems Reporting Resolutions These referred to machine parts that were not manufactured correctly and attention was needed to bring the parts back into tolerance. As you can see in eight months Vanguard had one PRR and this was one of the bogus parts that was sent to the inspection lab and came back correct.

Bill Blasko sent an e-mail to Vanguard on March 20, 2003 stating that the team wanted an elite group of suppliers capable of achieving quality, delivery, and pricing goals that Vanguard was not able to achieve. By their own records Vanguard Die and Machine more than achieved the goals set by the team, but we surpassed their expectations. The e-mails and graphs that Vanguard received from the team was supplied to Jerry of Delphi's legal department. It was obvious that Vanguard Die and Machine was sabotaged by Dean Hansen and Bill Blasko. If Jerry actually read all of the information that Vanguard had furnished Delphi's legal department it was obvious by eliminating Vanguard ability to quote on new work and continue manufacturing parts that were on Vanguard blankets cost Delphi millions of dollars.

Close to the same time that Vanguard Die and Machine was securing blankets in the make die area, we also had an opportunity to quote on a large volume of details in the assembly die area. A problem must have occurred in the purchasing of assembly die details in Warren, Ohio because the purchasing was transferred to Mississippi. When Vanguard first receive a package to quote the origin was quite surprising. The person in Mississippi who was handling the purchasing was Marie Jones. In the beginning things went well for Vanguard Die and Machine, Marie Jones, was very cordial and professional. The quoting of these blankets occurred before Vanguard Distributors came on the scene. Again, the main reason for this opportunity to present itself was that Vanguard Die and Machine prices and our reputation for doing quality work was excellent. Having these kinds of credentials allowed Vanguard to be placed on the preferred bidders list in the assembly die area. This gave Vanguard the opportunity to quote on the blankets.

The quoting process was similar to what we experienced in the past. After receiving the blanket package to quote, Vanguard would submit our cost back to Delphi. The prices would be reviewed and target prices would be sent back to the vendor, Delphi would go two to three rounds until one vendor was left. Quoting this way gave each vendor an opportunity to secure work if they were the last company with the lowest prices. Using this process gave Vanguard an opportunity to secure many. blankets and thousands of parts. The vendor with the lowest bid received contracts with a lifespan of two years. Most of the blankets had details with high-volume, as much as 100 parts a month for each detail. There were hundreds of details on some of these blankets. Vanguard was the lowest bidder on the majority of these blankets and with the high-volume, over time they were worth millions and millions of dollars. After securing blankets in the make die area, along with blankets in the assembly die area, Vanguard felt the future that lay ahead for us was secure.

As time went on, the use of these blankets in the assembly die area did not materialize. Vanguard was given an estimate of the usage that Delphi would be purchasing each month and year. This estimate was usually based on the previous years usage. Vanguard was encouraged to build an inventory of parts based on a percentage of the total usage. Over a period of time Vanguard built an inventory on each and every detail that was on our blankets. Having completed all the requests made by Delphi, Vanguard was expecting a reasonable flow of work from the blankets in the assembly die area. There must have been problems in the purchasing department, because the flow of work that Vanguard was expecting turned into a trickle. We would make calls to Delphi's purchasing department concerning the lack of orders. The purchasing department referred us to the process engineer in the assembly die area his response was the usage of these parts was low at this time but when the usage picks up Delphi would use the vendor who had the details on their blankets. Having high expectations for these blankets turned into a major letdown. The purchasing department was pleased with our pricing so every couple of years Delphi would renew our blankets. Even though the orders were few, something was better than nothing.

This policy went on for years. Every once in a while Vanguard would receive an order for a large quantity of parts, then, there would be nothing. It seemed quite out of the ordinary for this to be happening. Later on Vanguard came to the conclusion that the engineer had gone on vacation or had taken time off and that left the awarding of the purchase orders to the purchasing department, where they utilized the blankets.

It was Vanguard's understanding that the engineer would receive the order, check to see if the parts were on a blanket, and if they were, issue the purchase order to that vendor. If the parts were not on blankets, a request would go out to different vendors for spot by pricing. It was our understanding that the engineer was the decision-maker for purchase orders that were under $10,000 and anything over $10,000 had to be signed off by the purchasing department. There were millions of dollars at stake, it was foolish to have an engineer have that kind of unregulated power. If not used correctly, that power could easily cost Delphi millions of dollars. As you will come to understand poor management and questionable ethics cost Delphi millions upon millions of dollars.

Vanguard started hearing that Delphi was using hundreds of our details consisting of thousands of parts. Dale Beck was the engineer in charge when we started hearing rumors about favoritism toward a certain vendor. It was about 2003 when Vanguard started pressing Dale Beck about the lack of purchase orders for parts on our blankets. We informed Dale Beck about the rumors we were hearing about him bypassing Vanguard blankets and issuing purchase orders to Dave Barnes of Barnes Tool in Meadville, Pennsylvania. Dale Beck assured Vanguard this was not happening and he was not purchasing our blanket parts from Dave Barnes.

We explained to Dale that Delphi's purchasing department requested Vanguard build an inventory of parts. Dale stated he was sorry, but that requests for our blanket parts were not forthcoming. We reminded Dale that Vanguard was in Delphi's Targets for Excellent Program, which should have entitled Vanguard to quote new tooling and assemblies. Dale's response was that he was aware of this and would issue new tooling quotes to Vanguard if he felt we were qualified. Not receiving orders and quotes from the assembly die area was very disturbing to Vanguard. Each time we approached Dale about the lack of orders his reply was that they were not using our blanket parts and we should send over a list of parts that we had in stock. Vanguard continually approached Dale about lack of orders and his reply was that they were not using our parts and we should send over a list of parts we had in stock. That was his standard reply. Using this approach every couple of months we thought Dale would at least honor some of our blankets. This approach didn't seem to be working.

There must have been a revelation with Dale, because Vanguard received a purchase order for a group of details. Thinking this was a crack in the wall at Delphi, the excitement soon ended because the purchase order had actually been issued to Barnes Tool of Meadville Pennsylvania. Every part on the purchase order was on Vanguard Die and Machine's blankets. The cost that Dave Barnes of Barnes Tool was receiving for the parts were two to three times more than what was on Vanguard's blankets. Having the purchase order addressed to Vanguard Die and Machine instead of Barnes Tool was a major blunder by Dale Beck. Now Vanguard had proof that Dale was bypassing Vanguard's blankets and issuing purchase orders to Dave Barnes of Barnes Tool. We immediately called Dale Beck and requested a reason why he was issuing purchase orders for parts on Vanguard's blankets to Dave Barnes. Dale Beck admitted that he was sending our work to Barnes Tool and he had the right to send any work to whomever he wanted, and he didn't care what I thought. We explained that the prices Delphi was paying Dave Barnes were two to three times more than what Vanguard was charging.

During our many conversations with Dale concerning the lack of orders and the bypassing of our blankets, Dale assured us he would honor our blankets, yet the parts were ordered from Barnes Tool, so requesting an inventory of our parts was just a joke. Dale shot back to me that he wasn't going to honor any blankets. My response to him was to ask why he was sending out for quotes and bypassing Vanguard's blankets, and told him he was the only buyer not honoring our blankets. Dale again stated that he was not going to honor our blankets. He didn't care what things cost, and that the operation of his department was at his discretion. When he slammed down the phone it could be heard across the room. His arrogance left us quite bewildered. Our thoughts were, what do we do now? Dale taking this attitude towards Vanguard's blankets and costing Delphi millions upon millions of dollars was quite shocking. Delphi was shutting down departments, selling off business-es, and sending work to Mexico in order to cut costs. Now you have Dale Beck's approach to business," I don't care what things cost and I'm not honoring your blankets".

Vanguard finally decided to check with who we thought was the head of purchasing, George Sorry. We felt that contacting George was going to be a cure-all for Vanguard and would stop the bleeding of millions of dollars in the assembly die area at Delphi. The telephone conversation with George was very cordial. When we brought up the fact that Dale and Dave Barnes were costing Delphi millions and millions of dollars because Dale not honoring Vanguard's blankets. George seemed to be concerned about the attitude Dale was taking regarding losing money in Delphi's troubled times. We parted ways with George giving me his assurance that he would be checking into the matter and getting back to Vanguard.

A few weeks went by without any communication from George. Vanguard tried to contact George many times, to no avail. It wasn't until much later that Vanguard was informed that Dave Barnes and George Sorry had a special relationship. Deeper into the book the reader will see how George Sorry assisted Dave Barnes in receiving an anti-competitive position that could have cost Delphi millions and millions of dollars. After many years at that position the legal Department of Delphi finally shut it down. George Sorry, being a carrier of the torch for the future of Delphi should have been concerned about the shareholders of Delphi's stock not his friend. Again Vanguard Die and Machine was set back by the lack of follow-up by George Sorry.

Remembering that I knew a person in management at Delphi, a call was made to Sam Haack. Part of Sam Haack's job at Delphi was being the manager over the molding area. I explained my position to Sam con-cerning our blankets not being honored by Dale Beck and the millions of dollars it was costing Delphi. Sam was quite surprised our blankets were not being honored by Dale Beck. Sam assured me that this was not the norm throughout Delphi. In most meetings with management that Sam attended saving money was a major priority. I asked Sam if he knew someone at Delphi that could assist Vanguard with this problem. Sam said he wasn't sure he could make my request happen but he would do his best.

Approximately one week later Vanguard received a call from Sam Haack. An appointment would be set up with a person in management named Richard Snyder. Sam and I talked and we agreed on a time and place where Rich, Sam, and I could meet and go over Vanguard's grievances.

Sam set the meeting up to take place at Delphi and we were to meet Rich at his office. One of Rich's positions at Delphi was overseeing Dale Beck's department. Upon entering Rich's office we all shook hands and exchanged pleasantries. Rich was a little standoffish, but he was at least cordial. I was thinking that Rich would be a little more receptive, since I was about to show him how a Delphi employee under his direction was costing Delphi millions of dollars. After the handshaking and greetings took place Sam Haack excused himself, saying he would be back later and that we should be able to settle this without him. Before coming to Delphi, a list of parts that were on Vanguard's blankets was assembled along with the cost that Vanguard was charging Delphi. This way Rich could make a comparison between Dave Barnes and Vanguard's cost, and by our account it was huge. After presenting this list to Richard Snyder his reaction was quite surprising. Rich promptly stated that he was not going to check on anything. Rich Snyder then changed the subject. Rich wanted to know whether Vanguard was accusing Dale Beck of taking bribes from Dave Barnes. This turn of events was quite surprising to me. My reply to Rich Snyder was that if Dale Beck was taking bribes from Dave Barnes of Barnes Tool this was not my call.

Again, I showed Rich the list of parts that Vanguard had assembled, so he could see that Dale Beck and Dave Barnes were costing Delphi millions of dollars. This was ignored by Rich and his thoughts turned back to pressuring Vanguard about bribes. We assured Rich we were not accusing anybody of taking bribes. But I did suggest more investigation should be done to clear the air. That didn't seem to satisfy Rich, because he asked me at least four more times if I had come to his office to accuse Dave Barnes and Dale Beck of any wrong doing. Each time I suggested to Rich to do his own investigation and come up with his own conclusion. This was not an area we wanted to get involved in, but it sure looked suspicious. It seemed that once Rich knew I was not going to formerly accuse Dale Beck and Dave Barnes of any wrongdoing he became very belligerent and aggressive toward me.

Rich stated that he didn't care if I was going to accuse Dale and Dave of any wrongdoing because he didn't want to hear about it. This was his department and Dale's job performance was just fine. Rich had the right to run his department the way he wanted. I again slid the list of parts over the desk toward Rich and brought up the fact that these parts were on Vanguard blankets and obtain through the bidding process. Dave Barnes had the same opportunity as Vanguard to quote on these blankets. Dave was not the low bidder so he was not awarded the blankets. Rich said he didn't care about blankets or prices; he was going to do things his way. Rich's reaction was quite surprising to me because millions of dollars of losses for Delphi were at stake. Not one time during the meeting did Rich say, Vanguard's quality was bad, or Vanguard's delivery was not acceptable. I'm sure Rich did an investigation of Vanguard and came to the conclusion that we were a quality shop. So why he was taking this position was quite bewildering.

My request that Rich accept the list of parts and check them out was an easy request from Vanguard. Rich raised his voice, and I followed suit. I'm not sure what Rich thought was going to happen, but I did know I came with nothing; the worst that could happen was going home with nothing. If Rich wanted to call security, let it happen, because I needed these blankets to be honored. Vanguard had built an inventory of parts that was suggested by purchasing. We were not going to lose tens of thousands of dollars of inventory because of favoritism.

The noise coming out of Rich's office must have reached Sam Haack, because he came rushing in and remarked that we should settle our differences a little more quietly. As soon as Sam Haack made an appearance, Rich's demeanor changed from night to day. Rich's voice became much more contained. I again gave the list of parts to Rich and also explained to Sam Haack that this list showed how Delphi was losing millions and millions of dollars in overpayments to Dave Barnes of Barnes Tool. This was happening with assistance from Dale Beck.

After refusing to accept the list of parts we originally presented in the beginning, Rich now had second thoughts. Rich now gladly accepted the list and said he would look into the matter and instruct Dale to use Vanguard's blanket prices to purchase parts in the future. Rich also stated that he would instruct Dale Beck that Vanguard Die and Machine will have the opportunity to quote on all new tooling in the assembly die area. This was a grueling meeting and I was glad when it was over. Everyone shook hands and called it a day.

Walking out of Delphi with Sam I thanked him for all the help and explained to him that I couldn't have done it without his assistance. Driving back to the shop, I couldn't help thinking back to how the meeting started and how the final conclusion was so surprising. It had been quite a day. An e-mail was received from Rich Snyder thanking Vanguard for our concerns over Delphi's expenditures. In that e-mail there was also an inquiry on how we had obtained pricing information. (This is generally confidential priority information). Vanguard shared this information with Richard Snyder on three parts which was just the tip of the iceberg since Vanguard had hundreds of high-volume parts on blankets for as much as nine years.

Part#8JHC 125
other vendors cost $159 each
Vanguard's cost $49 each

$110 each difference when Vanguard started receiving orders for these parts the yearly quantity was approximately 700 pieces a year with a cost savings of approximately $77,000 a year for approximately 6 years Delphi overpaid approximately $462,000 for one part.

Part number 8JK the 153
other vendors cost $86 each
Vanguard's cost $39 each
$47 difference per part

Part number 8JKB153
other vendors cost $100 each
Vanguard's cost $39 each
$61 difference per part

Richard Snyder never showed any concerns about the prices Vanguard submitted to him, so we assumed that everything was correct. Over the years many of the high volume details were ordered hundreds of times costing Delphi millions and millions of dollars. The relationship between Dave Barnes and Dale Beck was a troubling alliance as far as Vanguard was concerned.

The day following the meeting between Richard Snyder, Sam Haack, and Vanguard at Delphi, we received a call from Dale Beck. Dale informed Vanguard that he was having problems with Richard Snyder and we were the cause of his problems. We informed Dale if he had honored Vanguard's blankets, and not lied about the use of our blankets, the problems would not have surfaced. He then informed us that the call was being made at the insistence of Rich. Honoring our blankets in the future would be standard practice and Vanguard would be receiving all quotes on new work.

For Rich to cause Dale that much grief, he must have checked on the parts we brought to his attention. Having checked on these parts and seeing the millions of dollars Delphi was losing, we assumed there would have been an investigation. The investigation could have been either internal or performed by an outside agency. When a company is losing millions of dollars due to a relationship between a buyer and vendor, you would think red flags would begin to wave. That doesn't mean there was any wrongdoing, but an investigation would have easily cleared the air.

Again, was this person in management looking out for Delphi employees and shareholders of Delphi's stock? I think not. When poor management takes hold of a company, employees and stockholders suffer the most. When bankruptcy takes place at a company, the unions and the employees take the blame. Poor management never comes into play. There were good employees that lost their jobs, health insurance, and their way of life because of Delphi's bankruptcy and the moving of jobs to Mexico and overseas. But as of September 2012 Richard Snyder still drives his car to work at Delphi and you can see Dale Beck walking into the plant. Thinking Vanguard had cleared a hurdle with Delphi management was a much better feeling than butting heads with them. As you will soon read, meeting delivery dates with good quality and especially lowering the cost on producing precision parts was not good enough for certain employees in management at Delphi. There were people who wanted Dave Barnes to flourish no matter what the cost to Delphi.

Vanguard Die and Machine started receiving quotes from Dale Beck at the same time we were receiving quotes from Jack Hagan, a corporate buyer. We learned that Jack Hagan was the purchasing agent to whom Dale Beck reported. The new quoting that Vanguard received from Dale Beck was for spot buys. This meant even though these parts were for large quantities and used quite often they were not put on blankets. Vanguard received an order from Dale for hundreds of precision parts. At first glance this order seemed to confirm that the problems between Dale and Vanguard were no longer a major issue. However, after looking at the purchase order and discovering the delivery date indicated the parts were already three days late. Vanguard contacted Dale Beck and questioned him about the delivery date on the purchase order. We requested a delivery date change and Dale assured Vanguard that the date was an oversight and not to be concerned. According to Dale it was the end of the year and he was spending down his budget. The parts on the purchase order we received would not be needed any time soon. After talking to Dale about this order we felt that our concerns were satisfied.

About one week later we received a call from Jack Hagan concerning the purchase order we had just received a week earlier from Dale. Jack was inquiring why this purchase order was late. We explained to Jack when we received the order, it was already three days late. I told him we discussed this issue with Dale and that Dale's response was; that the late delivery on the purchase order was nothing to be concerned about. It was just the result of a slight oversight on his part. Jack Hagan informed us it was Dale Beck who had called complaining about the order being late. Dale wanted to cancel the order with Vanguard and reallocate the purchase order to Dave Barnes. I guessed our problems with Dale have not come to a conclusion yet.

We explained to Jack Hagan the problems we have been having with Dale. Rehashing the meeting that took place between Rich, Sam, and me seemed to clear up a few points with Jack. We also pointed out to Jack the relationship between Dave Barnes and Dale Beck had cost Delphi millions and millions of dollars. I questioned Jack to see if we needed to contact Richard Snyder again. Jack seemed to understand the problem and informed us to do the best we could on delivery and he would keep Dale off our backs. After all the problems that Dale had with Vanguard and Rich Snyder you would assume that he would do everything he could to stay out of the spotlight. For Dale to go to this length to continue to divert work to Dave Barnes, upper management must have been protecting Dale. Most of this tooling eventually was transferred to Mexico and giving bad delivery dates and complaining at meetings about Vanguard's so-called late delivery was a standard practice in Mexico. I guess Dave Barnes had the Mexicans by the short hairs too.

Vanguard started receiving quotes for dies and assemblies from Jack Hagan in 2004, and these were major contracts worth millions of dollars. These large blankets were quoted at a minimum of three rounds until the company that was left was the lowest bidder. As we have discussed in the past, this method took all of the game playing and favoritism out of awarding the blankets. Vanguard Die and Machine had the latest technology along with very modern machinery, seven wire EDM machines and seven machining centers. Very few jobs shops our size had the quantity and quality of machinery we did. Vanguard's investment in this machinery paid off, because we could quote much cheaper than most other companies. The majority of the blankets that Jack Hagan was handling went to Vanguard Die and Machine. Having been awarded most of the blankets for the dies and assemblies, we came to know Nicole Smith.

Nicole Smith was the supervisor of the department that received the assemblies and dies that Vanguard was producing. Dave Barnes was manufacturing these assemblies and dies before the open bidding process was in place. Dave Barnes had every opportunity to acquire these dies and assemblies, but the failure of Dave Barnes quoting was a feather in Vanguard's hat. This did not stop his buddies at Delphi from doing everything they could to funnel work to him; the cost meant nothing. The bypassing of Vanguard's blankets by Dale Beck to Dave Barnes was not going to take place again.

Vanguard's first meeting with Nicole was a cautious one, because this was the first time these dies and assemblies were being completed by an outside vendor. Individual parts were usually built separately, by different vendors. After the completion of the individual parts, they were shipped to the assembly die area at Delphi. The assembly and the debugging of the dies would be completed in-house at Delphi. It was a major step for Delphi to have dies and assemblies built and de bugged by an outside vendor. The reason for caution on Delphi's part was that many of these these dies were resold to outside suppliers. In the beginning Nicole was not in favor of Vanguard building and debugging the dies.

The main reason she was apprehensive was, that Dale Beck and Dave Barnes were running a negative campaign against Vanguard. Dave

Barnes had the same opportunity to acquire these blankets as Vanguard. Quoting less than Vanguard would have solved the problem. Not being able to compete against Vanguard in an open quoting system did not stop Dave Barnes. Dave wanted to maintain this work in his shop, but at a much higher cost. We heard through the grapevine, that Dale and Dave had met with Nicole trying to convince her to stay with Dave Barnes. Vanguard was very fortunate(this time) to have employees at Delphi that only looked out for the best interest of their employer and not for special interest groups or favorite vendors.

My last two experiences in the past with buyers at Delphi have not turned out to be very productive. Fortunately the tide changed when Jack Hagan stepped up and supported Vanguard. We contacted Jack and relayed to him our concerns about Dale Beck and Dave Barnes. Jack said not to worry; we were low bid so Vanguard will receive the purchase order. The sad reality was that, if you bucked Dave Barnes and his friends in management at Delphi, your length of employment at Delphi was terminal. Being a supporter of low prices, quality work, and on time delivery is what Vanguard brought to the table. This made all the vendors that Vanguard was competing against, stand up and take notice. Vanguard was here and you better sharpen your pencils. Some employees in management wanted a different ending. It seemed they were more concerned about helping Dave Barnes than saving money for their own troubled company (Delphi).

Getting back to the employees that supported Vanguard, a few months after Stan Haack set up and attended the meeting between Rich Snyder and Vanguard, Sam was put in an uncomfortable position causing him to take early retirement. Jack Hagan put his job on the line by supporting what was best for Delphi. He supported Vanguard's low prices and quality work all the way to Troy Michigan. Even though it was the right thing to do, and saved Delphi millions of dollars, Jack's head was put on the chopping block and he was terminated. Nicole became a very strong supporter of Vanguard because of quality and pricing.

Nicole and Jack both took a chance by backing Vanguard when management in Troy Michigan became involved.

Even though Nicole helped save Delphi millions of dollars, she was given a choice by Delphi management: take a pay cut or leave. She chose the exit route. Vanguard had another strong supporter; Dick Winner who lived and worked in Troy, Michigan. One of Dick's jobs was overseeing areas in Mexico that Vanguard serviced. Dick was a very loyal Delphi employee who forced Warren, Ohio management and Mexico's management to back down and accept Vanguard as a supplier, saving Delphi millions of dollars. Roadblocks were placed in front of Vanguard by Delphi's management only for the purpose of enhancing the wealth of their friends at the cost of millions of dollars in Delphi's overpayments. Dick's dedication to Delphi helped destroy many of those roadblocks. The sad thing about life is that even when you are young, tragic turns of fate can put a dark face on future years. At a young age Dick had a brain aneurysm.

Dale Beck was still portraying Vanguard as a company that didn't have the ability to handle the assembly die project. Dale was giving Vanguard deliveries for projects that were unattainable or late even before we received the purchase order. Dale would approach Jack Hagan and Nicole to complain about poor deliveries and insisted that Dave Barnes be awarded the assembly die project. Knowing the alliance that Dale Beck had with Dave Barnes, Jack, and Nicole turned a deaf ear to Dale. Not having much success with Jack and Nicole, Dale turned to Joe Pack.

Joe Pack was an engineer involved in the design of the assembly dies. Dale approached Joe about the quality of parts that Vanguard was furnishing to the assembly die area. As Joe was investigating the complaint that Dale presented to him, Joe decided to give Vanguard a call. He wanted to know what Dale's problem was. Joe knew that Vanguard had been awarded the assembly die blankets and hadn't heard any complaints other than those from Dale. As Joe put it, "Dale was constantly trying to undermine Vanguard." Along with this undermining Dale was always pushing to recommend Barnes Tool as the primary supplier for the assembly die blankets. Joe was questioning me to see if there was a problem between Dale and Vanguard because he felt there was more going on between Dale and Dave Barnes than met the eye.

During the telephone conversation, I brought up the fact Dale had been bypassing our blankets and issuing purchase orders to Dave Barnes. This practice lasted for years. The purchase orders that Dale Beck issued to Dave had a value of 2 to 3 times greater than the cost on Vanguard blankets. This practice cost Delphi millions and millions of dollars. We also discussed the meeting between Richard Snyder, myself, and Sam Haack and how, during that meeting Richard Snyder's interest turned to bribes between Dale Beck and Dave Barnes.

Joe said that those concerns were out of his jurisdiction and that he wouldn't comment on that particular subject. **Those** were decisions made by upper management. Joe assured Vanguard that Dale's complaints were not realistic and he advised Vanguard to just continue in the direction we were taking and everything would be fine.

In the middle of 2004 Vanguard placed another complaint with Rich Snyder concerning Dale's undermining of Vanguard's ability to perform the work on the assembly dies. Dale's complaints went to Jack Hagan, Joe Pack, and Nicole Smith. Each time, Dale was trying to portray Vanguard in a negative light and was asking for an endorsement of Dave Barnes as the preferred supplier of the assembly dies. If this did happen, it would again cost Delphi millions of dollars. Rich Snyder's answer to our complaint was to in informed Vanguard that he was no longer in the assembly die business in Ohio. The assembly dies were transferred to Mexico, with the exception of some activity in Nicole's area. It was around this time that Vanguard received a notification from Delphi that the assemblies were going to be transferred to Mexico. The purchasing agent and engineer from Mexico were coming to Warren, Ohio. A meeting was set up between José (the purchasing agent) and John Brown (an engineer) with Vanguard Die and Machine. Upon meeting with José and John they seemed nice enough and a decision was made to go out to lunch. Jack Hagan was in charge of the meeting to ensure everything went smoothly. During the luncheon, John informed us he had reviewed our work on the assembly dies with Nicole and her recommendation was quite impressive. He also knew that Vanguard was the only vendor that built and de bugged the assembly dies. It was suggested by José that Vanguard was probably going to be the primary supplier of assemblies along with the extra spare parts that were going to be needed. As the meeting came to an end we at Vanguard felt we were in a good position to continue building the assemblies and spare parts for Mexico.

Not long after that meeting Vanguard had a question concerning a purchase order with Nicole. After contacting Nicole and resolving our problems, out of nowhere Nicole stated that Dave Barnes and his foreman were in Mexico for three days. At that time, the significance of Dave spending time in Mexico didn't register with Vanguard. Approximately two more times, the subject of Dave and his foreman spending time in Mexico was relayed to Vanguard by Nicole. This still did not ring a bell or cause any alarms to go off, but not long after, Barnes Tool was awarded the Mexico blankets to build the assemblies.

This was quite a shock to Vanguard because we felt Vanguard was on the right track to at least get an opportunity to quote on the assemblies. Having lost the blankets to Barnes Tool, we did a little checking and heard Barnes had been awarded the blankets without following the quoting process. We knew one thing, whatever process they used to select the vendor, Vanguard was not included. Even though upper management knew they lost millions upon millions of dollars through the relationship between Dale Beck and Dave Barnes, this did not seem to matter. This is another betrayal by management of the employees that were laid-off, lost their homes, health insurance, pensions, and a middle-class way of life. This was a slap in the face to all shareholders and employees of Delphi. The success and future of Dave Barnes of Barnes Tool was more important than the shareholders at Delphi This move said screw the little guy.

Management at most companies is expected to represent their share-holders. Management at Delphi had lost their way, and bankruptcy was inevitable. The profitability of a company would be in jeopardy if favoritism and friendships came into play when awarding contracts. Delphi could easily go bankrupt if the majority of their departments followed these guidelines. As you can see, Dave Barnes of Barnes Tool was more important than Delphi shareholders or laid-off employees, some of whom lost everything. In upcoming chapters the readers come to understand how unethical or stupid Delphi management had become. The things that management did to enhance Dave Barnes's wealth was unprecedented, and 99% percent of companies would not even consider it, let alone let it happen, but the dies, assemblies, and spare parts were going to Mexico and the blankets were being awarded to Dave Barnes.

From that time on, Vanguard tried to encourage José and John Brown to give Vanguard an opportunity to quote the tooling. Vanguard assured José and John Brown that we could save Delphi millions of dollars. The loss of money didn't seem to bother José or John Brown even though Delphi was rapidly closing in on bankruptcy.

Vanguard was receiving some purchase orders from Delphi Mexico. The purchase orders originated from José, with the parts being received by John Brown. The majority of the purchase orders Vanguard received from Delphi Mexico had delivery dates of two days to six days, even though quantities were between 200 and 400 pieces per detail. Since we were receiving standard purchase orders that had short delivery dates, we wondered whether Dave Barnes's purchase orders also had short delivery dates. This seemed to be the standard pattern throughout Delphi's management toward Vanguard Die and Machine. The sabotaging of Vanguard move from Warren, Ohio to Mexico, just to make Barnes Tool look good and to ensure that they remained the primary supplier at Delphi Mexico for the assemblies.

As usual, contacting John and José to get the delivery dates changed was impossible. It seemed after Vanguard received purchase orders that were inconsistent with normal business practices José and John were not available. Neither one would respond to e-mails or telephone calls. Even though José and John were unresponsive, Vanguard built the tooling and shipped as quickly as possible, but being forced to use their erroneous delivery dates, we were usually late. Most of the time Vanguard had part of the order in stock, which we would ship out as quickly as possible. Then we would follow-up with the balance. Purchase orders from Mexico dropped to a trickle, and contacting John or José to inquire about any problem was usually impossible.

Vanguard continuously tried to contact Mexico finally a response from José. We inquired about the problem of Vanguard not receiving any purchase orders. His response was that Vanguard had too many late deliveries. We explained to José that meeting three day delivery and six day delivery on hundreds of parts was impossible. José assured Vanguard that he would check into the matter and get back to us, but receiving a call or an e-mail from José never took place.

José and John knew that Vanguard had impossible delivery dates, but that didn't stop them from going to meetings and complaining about Vanguard's failure to meet delivery and therefore the work should be going to Barnes Tool.

The purchase orders that Vanguard was receiving at this time were for spare parts rather than for dies. Vanguard brought to the attention of Jack Hagan, José, John, Nicole, and Pedro Garcia that awarding Dave Barnes the blanket contracts for the assembly dies without competitive bidding was costing Delphi millions of dollars. Finally we were able to set up a meeting in Mexico to explore the possibilities of opening up the bidding process for the assembly dies. This meeting would give Vanguard the opportunity to express our concerns and assure Delphi that a savings of $700-$800 per assembly would be provided by Vanguard. The meeting was held around July 2006 with José, John, Pedro, and three other people with whom we were not familiar. Pedro was in charge of the meeting, but informed us in the beginning that he had another meeting to attend. He felt sure José, John, and Vanguard would be able to come to a conclusion that would satisfied everyone. As the meeting progressed José and John agreed that, going out for competitive bidding was in the best interest for Delphi Mexico. José assured us that the bidding process would take place in about four to six weeks. Once again this never happened, and our e-mails and telephone calls went unanswered.

Pedro Garcia was José and John's supervisor. He knew about the savings that Vanguard presented to José and John. The savings that Vanguard presented was ignored even though it was worth millions. One commodity that Delphi had an abundance of was piss poor management. Our only recourse was to go back to Nicole and Jack to see if they had any suggestions. Jack and Nicole both said, they would go back to George Sorry and explained to him about José and John favoring Dave Barnes even though Vanguard was making almost the exact same die in Warren, Ohio. Vanguard was willing to cut the cost by $700-$800 per completed die. With Delphi buying between 700 to 1000 assemblies a year over time the savings would be in the millions.

After Jack explained the situation to George Sorry his response was, he would look into it. As time went on Jack said, he had mentioned it to George a few more times and still hadn' t received any feedback. Nicole said, she had talked to George a couple of times about the overpayment to Dave Barnes by Dale Beck in the Warren assembly die area that costs Delphi millions of dollars. She expressed concern to George that this was happening again, only now with John, José, and Dave Barnes because of John and José's refusal to go out for competitive bidding.

Nicole informed Vanguard that she had worn out her welcome with George Sorry. She was thinking if she continued to bring this subject up to George, she could lose her job, but she felt if there was any other way she could assist us she would.

It wasn't too long after this that I approached Nicole about Vanguard putting together a proposal for the dies and asked if she would submitt it to Mexico for Vanguard. We knew putting together a proposal and submitting it to John and José without a formal request it would be ignored. But having Nicole's name on the proposal would carry much more weight. Vanguard put the proposal together and Nicole submitted it to José and John. Nicole seemed quite excited about the proposal and said, "let's keep our fingers crossed and hope they acknowledge the savings that Vanguard has created in the Warren area so Mexico can also take advantage of the savings.".

Originally our thoughts were the savings would be around $400-$500 per assembly, but after review Vanguard was able to up the savings to $700-$800 per assembly. With 1000 assemblies per year, the savings would be between $700,000 and $800,000 a year. This does not take into account all the other dies and assemblies that Vanguard was excluded from quoting. This proposal must have landed on blind eyes, because José and John never showed any interest in saving Delphi money. Having Dave Barnes receive an extra $700,000-$800,000 a year must have met with José and John's approval.

We never did receive a clear answer from Nicole about why she went out of Her way to support Vanguard.

Nicole never went out to lunch with anyone from Vanguard. Over the years we only had a few meetings with her and they all took place in her office at Delphi. Nicole was a devoted employee to Delphi and her department. Setting high standards for quality was a priority to her with cost always being a major concern. The customer's needs always took center stage. Whatever the needed, Nicole tried to make it happen. There were times when Vanguard would received a telephone call from her department requesting a part to be rushed or early delivery on a die, anything to satisfy a customer's needs. The lies that Dale Beck and Dave Barnes were spreading about Vanguard and the overpayments to Barnes Tool, costing her department millions and millions of dollars, might have been Nicole's motivation to assist Vanguard.

It wasn't too long after our proposal to José and John was ignored that Vanguard received a call from Jack Hagan. Jack said there were people at Delphi headquarters in Troy, Michigan who could help Vanguard secure the assembly die business in Mexico. He gave us a name so we could begin our search. Finding the right person in Troy that could assist Vanguard did not turn out to be an easy task. If that person was out there, he and Nicole would support Vanguard in any way possible. The name we received from Jack was going to be our starting point. After the phone call to the recommended person, and presenting our position, he informed us that he was not the right person but he proceeded to give us another name and wished Vanguard good luck.

Contacting the new person still left Vanguard without the correct employee in management that could assist us. The employees in management at Delphi headquarters tried to be helpful, but they didn't know exactly which way to direct us. After about a month of trying to locate a helpful person in Troy Michigan without much success, the name of a person we had met in Mexico came to mind. When we had our first meeting in Mexico with José and John we were introduced to Rick Cohan. At that time Rick happened to be José and John's supervisor.

We knew Rick to be an honest person because he was involved in the firing of John's predecessor (Frank Roddick) for taking bribes. He was technically fired for improper use of a computer, but we later learned it was for receiving improper gifts. Vanguard had little contact with Frank because he ignored our requests to open up dialogue so that Vanguard would be able to receive future purchase orders, but then, out of the clear blue sky, Frank suddenly wanted Vanguard as a supplier for Delphi Mexico. Frank sent over a couple of large quotes hoping Vanguard and Mexico could work out an agreement so we could start producing these parts and become a permanent supplier for Delphi Mexico. The cost that Frank was shooting for was quite a bit lower than our normal pricing, but hoping to open up the doors in Delphi Mexico, Vanguard agreed.

The termination of Frank's employment in Mexico followed soon after. Frank's head was on the chopping block and he knew it, so he thought bringing Vanguard into the quoting arena might save his skin; it didn't. The purchase order we received from Frank was a losing proposition for Vanguard, but we honored the order for a year. The employees that followed Frank were John and José. Rick Cohan was there when the transition took place. Rick was transferred to another Delphi area in the United States. When that happened professionalism and integrity left Mexico.

Contacting Rick and explaining our plight to him and getting his reaction was our next step. After our initial conversation with Rick, he stated, a little research was needed to see if a person who could help us existed, and he would get back to us either way. Within a week Vanguard received a call from Rick with the name of a person that we should contact. His name was Dick Winner and we were hoping his assistance would be available.

Dick was located at Delphi's headquarters in Troy, Michigan and part of his duties was overseeing the Mexico operations of dies, assemblies, and spare parts. Vanguard's initial conversation with Dick was cordial, but we could tell he was a little apprehensive with our description of the problem in Mexico. He agreed to hold a meeting with Vanguard. At the first meeting, I brought along the dies that Vanguard was making and the dies that Barnes's Tool was making for the Delphi Mexico. There was only a slight difference, such as between Vanguard's dies and Barnes's dies. We informed Dick about our initial quote to José and John through Nicole with José and John not responding. The price savings to Delphi Mexico for a completed die was approximately $700-$800 each. The yearly savings was considerable at approximately $700,000-$800,000 a year. This did not include all the spare parts, subassemblies, and dies that Vanguard was excluded from quoting. The savings could have been in the millions. Dick took the information that Vanguard presented at the meeting, with the assurance he would be reporting back to us. A few days went by, then a week without any contact from Dick.

The passing of a couple of weeks took place before we received any correspondence from Dick. When the telephone did ring it was a call from a very irate Dick Winner who accused Vanguard of lying to him about where the Mexico assemblies were being built. In our first meeting that took place with Dick, it was brought up that the dies were being built in Meadville, Pennsylvania by Dave Barnes of Barnes Tool. Dick contacted Mexico to discuss with John the cost of the assembly dies and the elimination of Vanguard from the bidding process. John's response to Dick was that Vanguard was not included in the bidding because they were only using Mexican sources at that time. The assemblies were being built in Mexico.

The normal procedure of a colleague requesting information from another colleague is that their correspondence is truthful. Why Dick didn't just dismiss Vanguard as not being informed properly is beyond me. Vanguard and Delphi were both lucky that Dick wanted to get to the truth. I assured Dick that we were certain the assembly dies and spare parts were being built in Meadville Pennsylvania by Dave Barnes. We suggested that Dick contact Jack Hagan or Nicole to get their input on the matter. I am guessing, but he must have talked to either Jack Hagan or Nicole or both because Vanguard received another call from Dick.

This time he confirmed that the spare parts and assembly dies were being built by Dave Barnes in Meadville, Pennsylvania and not in Mexico. Dick didn't say whether there was a breakdown in communication between John and himself or whether John had just plain lied. Dick brought up another problem that John had, it was with Vanguard's late deliveries. Being in business for any length of time, problems were certain to arise at different times. No vendor wants to upset the company that buys their services. Long-term associations with a company makes it easier for your business to operate. Having contracts with large multinational companies is an even bigger plus. One of the big advantages of doing business with Delphi was the payment of money.

Delphi always paid on time. Whatever the agreed pay structure was, Delphi lived up to their end of the bargain. Doing business with smaller companies sometimes had its own set of problems. Being paid on time is the main drawback. Being in business with a dentistry background is a plus, because receiving payment for your services from smaller companies is sometimes like pulling teeth.

In 2006 Vanguard had a twenty two year ongoing relationship with Delphi. To continually have late deliveries that interfered with production would not have been acceptable to Delphi. On the surface the assertion by John that Vanguard continually had unacceptable delivery would be a little suspect. If that was true it would be difficult to understand how Vanguard had lasted twenty two years. In the telephone conversation Vanguard had with Dick concerning the late delivery problems, his tone was much milder. I'm sure that Dick felt there was more to the situation than John was presenting.

My explanation to Dick about the late deliveries indicated problems at different times do exist and this is unavoidable. To make sure that Delphi was not left without parts Vanguard made every effort to get at least a partial delivery on time and then follow-up with the balance. This was not an everyday occurrence. Dealing with hundreds of precision parts on a single purchase order, with short delivery dates, problems do arise. Vanguard's biggest concern was that John would constantly give Vanguard short delivery dates. One day delivery to two weeks delivery was not uncommon and Vanguard would sometimes receive orders that were already late. Having the association with Dick to help determine what were lies and what was the truth from John was a lucky draw for Vanguard. We sent out approximately ten to fifteen purchase orders to Troy, Michigan to show Dick how John manipulated the system. Vanguard conveyed to Dick how we would e-mail and make calls complaining about receiving unfair delivery dates from John. These communications with John landed on deaf ears and blind eyes because we never received an e-mail or phone call from John to review delivery problems. When Dick received our list of bogus delivery dates, he again contacted John to get his assessment of the facts. John, not being able to explain away the bogus delivery dates on purchase orders, he again found more to complain about to Dick concerning Vanguard. John next came up with a list of purchase orders that he said were late.

Vanguard's files were checked and, as usual, what John was saying was totally untrue. Vanguard sent back to Dick a list of delivery dates showing when these particular parts were shipped. Our parts were shipped by UPS and, with complaints of late delivery by Delphi being nonexistent, Vanguard assumed the orders had arrived in Delphi El Paso without a problem. Delivering to El Paso was the first stop for Vanguard's parts with the final destination being Jarez, Mexico. To make the trip across the border a truck would pick up the packages in El Paso and transport them across the border to Juarez Mexico. The only conclusion that Dick and I could come up with was that 95% percent of the parts that Vanguard manufactured went into inventory, so their use was not an immediately need. The assemblies could be left on the dock for a week to a month before these assemblies were needed. After a need became apparent a truck would transfer the assemblies from Delphi El Paso across the board to Juarez, Mexico. John would use the late delivery by the truck as the official delivery date. This was only a guess Dick and I made because the delivery date that John was concerned about were clearly on time. Dick was trying to be as professional as he could, but I could tell he was very upset with John's lies and how he was trying to discredit Vanguard.

The only thing that John didn't complain about was the quality of Vanguard work, so I brought that subject up to Dick. He said that in the initial conversation with John, the quality was the only thing he didn't complain about concerning Vanguard, so Dick pressed John about Vanguard's quality. He was quite surprised John's assessment of Vanguard's quality was not negative. Vanguard informed Dick that, while we were proving John was a liar and he was in the process of trying to sabotage Vanguard, he was going to meetings and complaining about Vanguard's delivery and not being the right vendor to take over the assembly dies and spare parts. We explained to Dick that it seemed like John's main goal was to have Dave Barnes of Barnes Tool be the sole supplier of the assemblies and spare parts in Juarez, Mexico. Even though Vanguard's cost was so much less than Dave Barnes's shop with the savings from Vanguard in the millions of dollars, the reaction from Dick was quite mild as he expressed his belief that everything would eventually work out.

While the problems between John, Dick and Vanguard Die and Machine were playing out, an employee in Mexico by the name of Tom Brown was evaluating Vanguard at Dick's request. Vanguard became aware of this evaluation in a later e-mail from Dick. After sifting through the lies and favoritism toward Dave Barnes by John, a conclusion finally had to be reached: Dick accepted our quote for the assemblies and spare parts which also opened up the doors for quotes that John excluded Vanguard from receiving. This took place in early January 2007, Vanguard was instructed to contact John and let him know when we could start receiving orders. Our call to John was immediate, with the explanation that Dick wanted Vanguard and John to work together so Delphi Mexico could start enjoying the savings.

Having out bid John's friend Dave Barnes we were not sure what reaction we would receive. Not only did we outbid Dave Barnes, but John was forced to open up the bidding process to Vanguard on all other dies, spare parts, and assemblies. This put Dave Barnes at a major disadvantage. John's attitude toward Vanguard was a little cold, but he insisted he would direct any new orders toward Vanguard. John also stated, their inventory was overloaded and it might be a while before any orders were forthcoming.

It was sometime in late January or early February that Vanguard was having a conversation with Nicole and at the end of the conversation it was brought up that Vanguard hadn't received any orders for assemblies from John in Mexico. Nicole offered to check on the status of the assemblies in Mexico and to our amazement, according to Nicole, John had placed an order for 400 assemblies to Dave Barnes. It was surprising to Vanguard that this had happened because using our figures this one order cost Delphi Mexico between $280,000 to $360,000. Vanguard again had to go back to Dick and explain to him that we were not receiving any orders for the assembly dies, nor had we received a hard copy of the blanket contracts.

It wasn't until April 2007 that we started receiving orders for the assembly dies. It wasn't too long after this that Vanguard was again receiving unattainable delivery dates from John. Dick was again contacted and informed that John was back to his old tricks of giving outrageous delivery dates for the assembly dies. A few days had passed when Vanguard received correspondence from Dick stating, this problem would not happen again and if we had any problems at all with John we were to contact him and he would take care of it immediately. A short time later, I happened to be talking to Dick, and I brought up the subject of John. I quizzed him as to how a large corporation that was struggling to get out of bankruptcy could employ a person like John who cost Delphi millions of dollars. Dick suggested to me that within six months there would be another person in his position. The changing of the guard in that position never took place. As of 2012 John was still working at that position.

While Dick was watching over John and the Mexican operation, Vanguard's problems with John were nonexistent. Vanguard received reasonable delivery dates from John and they were met. We never had any complaints about quality, and our pricing was always very competitive. The next two years were uneventful. Vanguard built many new types of dies and assemblies for Delphi Mexico. Vanguard saved Delphi millions of dollars. It could've been millions more if John would have opened the bidding process sooner. Due to John's questionable favoritism toward Dave Barnes, Delphi's losses were in the millions.

In 2009 our blankets were coming to an end, and with the savings that Delphi was receiving from Vanguard, we were sure the blankets would be renewed but this never happened. Vanguard was informed by John that the assemblies were being phased out and everything was being built in Mexico. Knowing John's past of having a difficult time with the truth, Vanguard decided to contact Dick again. The phone calls and e-mails that we directed to Dick went unanswered. To us this was very surprising because in the past Dick had been so helpful and honest. Our thoughts were, Dick had been transferred or left Delphi for greener pastures. Either way we never had contact with Dick again.

It wasn't until approximately three years later, when Vanguard was working with the legal department at Delphi, that we met with Jerry.

Our association with Jerry and the legal Department at Delphi will be discussed in more detail at the end of the book. During a meeting with Jerry it was discussed how Vanguard was saving Delphi Mexico millions of dollars compared to the cost Barnes Tool was charging. We explained to Jerry how Dick was a great help to Vanguard in obtaining those blankets but in 2009 when our blankets were not renewed by John, Vanguard tried to contact Dick without success. Jerry then informed Vanguard the reason why we were not able to contact Dick was because he had a brain aneurysm in 2009 and no longer worked at Delphi. This was quite a shock to Vanguard because after meeting with Dick and having correspondence with him through e-mails and phone conversation you could tell that Dick was not only a loyal Delphi employee but a nice honest guy. Sorry to say we never did find out the final outcome of Dick pertaining to his health. Whether the loss of the blankets in Mexico was tied to the health issues that Dick had, never became clear. It did seem like an odd coincidence that both happened very close to each other. Vanguard lost the blankets in Mexico but a couple times a year Vanguard would receive spot buys from Mexico.

The renewal of these blankets by John did not take place so there was not enough work to retain many of the employees that were working on these projects. The downside of owning your own business is that when times are slow and layoffs have to take place, it is very difficult when you know the chances of being called back are slim. The employees that completed their apprenticeships and received their journeyman's card were able to secure good jobs. Some employees lacked skills and had a difficult time securing employment. These were sad times for employees at Vanguard Die and Machine. While building these assembly dies, fixtures, spare parts, and specialty dies for Delphi Mexico, Vanguard had accumulated many spare parts. Mexico's need for many of these spare parts was still active, but we were not successful in getting John to purchase these parts from Vanguard. We tried to contact John concerning these parts many times. At first we offered to sell the parts at our blanket cost or if they were buying the parts from a lower cost vendor we would match that cost. That didn't work, so we lowered our cost just to clean out our inventory. This offer was also ignored. We later learned Dave Barnes was receiving purchase orders from John for parts Vanguard had in stock and paying a higher cost. I guess this is big business at work or maybe big business translated means" whose your buddy", the hell with the cost. Having dealt with employees in upper management at Delphi in the past, to proceed and try to get any support for Vanguard was a waste of time. As you will learn later, what management was sanctioning concerning Dave Barnes was absolutely unconscionable. Jerry said to me, the unethical handling of certain projects by Delphi's upper management favoring Dave Barnes showed certain employees in upper management were going to be retrained. That's just what an investor likes to hear: poor management that needs retraining.

Having lost the business in the make die area due to the sabotaging by Dean Hansen, Bill Blasko, and Larry Bolan, and losing 90% percent of the business in Mexico, our last bit of work for Delphi was outside sales. This department was for the assembly dies in Warren, Ohio and the supervisor was Nicole. At this time Vanguard had about 90% percent of the work in this area. Nicole was one of the employees at Delphi that was instrumental in Vanguard receiving the blankets from Mexico along with Jack Hagan and Dick Winner. Nicole's main goal as a Delphi supervisor was to have her department operate as efficiently and economically as possible. Vanguard was the supplier with the lowest prices, along with quality and delivery helped her achieve that goal. It was Nicole's Department that Dale Beck was associated with when Dave Barnes was being overpaid millions of dollars due to Dale's lack of ethics. The money that Dave Barnes was overpaid came out of Nicole's budget and she was furious when this came to light. Vanguard Die and Machine must have lived up her expectations, because Vanguard serviced her department for about fifteen years. Being a loyal employee to Delphi along with helping Vanguard secure the blankets with Delphi Mexico was obviously a kiss of death for Nicole. In 2009 Nicole was asked to take a cut in pay to retain her job or she would have to leave Delphi, even though she helped save Delphi millions of dollars. Not wanting to take a pay cut she decided to move on.

After the departure of Nicole, there was a void in the leadership in her department. It may come as a major shock but Dave Barnes's other company Triangle Commodity Group was given the task of overseeing the assembly dies and spare parts for outside sales in Warren, Ohio. Dave Barnes was advanced to this task even though he and Dale Beck had a special relationship that cost Delphi millions and millions of dollars. Management knew that this problem existed but apparently this meant nothing. Dave Barnes also had a special relationship with John, as was confirmed by Dick during our negotiations with Delphi Mexico. The special relationship between Dave Barnes and John cost Delphi millions of dollars and management knew this, but again it's not being a good loyal vendor that saves a company millions of dollars that matters but rather, it's who you know that seems to be the main priority with Delphi's upper management.

With the help of Sam Hack, Vanguard was able to force Rich Snyder to acknowledge that Dale Beck was bypassing Vanguard's blankets and moving the work to Dave Barnes, costing Delphi millions and millions of dollars. Having the help of Nicole, Jack Hagan, and Dick Winner, Vanguard was able to secure the blankets for the assembly dies in Mexico saving Delphi millions. When these things happened it eliminated Dave Barnes from making millions of dollars in overpayments by Dale Beck in Warren, Ohio and John in Mexico. Now Delphi promoted Dave Barnes, my competitor, to decide Vanguard's future at Delphi. Delphi calls this good management, what a bunch of assholes!

Now having Dave Barnes as my boss, the life expectancy of Vanguard looked very grim. Sam Haack was gone. Dick Winner was gone. Jack Hagan was on his way out. Now Nicole was gone. The only employees left were Dave Barnes and his allies. Now you know why Delphi had such a difficult time coming out of bankruptcy.

Our first crisis arose when Triangle Commodity Group wanted to extend some blankets Vanguard had in Warren, Ohio. The many parts on the blankets generated very few orders so it was not going to be possible to maintain a reasonable workforce. To refresh our readers, Triangle Commodity Group was owned by Dave Barnes and the supervisor was Bill Blasko. Bill Blasko along with Dean Hansen was at the forefront of Vanguard Distributors successful effort to sabotage Vanguard Die and Machine's presence in the make die area.

Triangle Commodity Group replaced Vanguard Distributors around 2005 with the support of George Sorry. When Vanguard was informed that Triangle Commodity Group was taking over the make die area, we called and expressed our concern to Jack Hagan that this was a conflict of interest. His reaction to my complaint was that, he had nothing to do with that decision. As Jack Hagan explained, it was George Sorry who handled the outsourcing of the die parts in the make die area for Delphi. George Sorry sent out for quotes to different companies and after receiving the quotes George approached Dave Barnes, (Vanguard Die and Machines competitor) to inquire if Dave could come in at a lower cost, even though this was clearly a conflict of interest, as Delphi's legal department eight years later agreed. After George and Dave worked out the details, Jack Hagan was told to push it through purchasing. My complaint to Jack Hagan was a waste of time because George was Jack's boss and he said he was just following orders.

Going back a few years Vanguard Distributors demanded that Vanguard Die and Machine take on a partner because Vanguard Distributors and Vanguard Die and Machine names were to similar, which was ridiculous. Now that roadblock is no longer there, Vanguard Die and Machine contacted Triangle Commodity Group to request that Vanguard be reinstated in the make die area. A call was made to Triangle Commodity Group and a conversation between Cindy Silo and Vanguard took place, with an e-mail that followed requesting to be reinstated in the make die area. As Dave Barnes could not compete against Vanguard in the make die area, and with the help of Sam Haack we took our work back from Dave Barnes in the assembly die area in Warren, Ohio, and with the help of Dick Winner, Dave Barnes was ousted and we were awarded the blankets in Delphi Mexico. I'm sure Triangle Commodity Group would gladly open up their arms to Vanguard who was their major competitor. With this kind of stupidity at Delphi management it's easy to understand why Delphi went bankrupt and employees lost their health insurance, their retirement, some people lost their homes and a way of life that supported their families

Getting back to the extension of some spare parts blankets controlled by Triangle Commodity Group, Bill Blasko requested a meeting with Vanguard concerning these blankets. During the meeting in 2009 we refreshed Bill Blasko's memory about Vanguard's past experience in the make die area. How Vanguard saved Delphi millions of dollars and by their own records we had at least 96% percent on time delivery and our quality was impeccable. We suggested that reinstatement of Vanguard in the make die area by Dave Barnes and Triangle Commodity Group would go a long way in convincing Vanguard to accept the extension of the spare parts blankets.

Reinstatement into the make die area didn't happen, so Vanguard turned down the extension of the spare parts blankets, hoping that the extra cost to Delphi of having another vendor manufacture these parts would open up some eyes at Delphi. What a bizarre thought: Delphi management having some brains?

Vanguard was running out of Delphi personnel with whom to register a complaint about Dave Barnes and his abnormal ties with Delphi management, which had already cost Delphi shareholders millions and millions of dollars.

Vanguard's complaints went to George Sorry, Bill Blasko, Cindy Silo, Dean Hansen, Pedro Garcia, Al Galloway, Dennis Gallagher, Sam house, Tom Brown, John Brown José, Rich Snyder, Dale Beck, Jerry Day, Will Jones, and Ken Sales. The feedback was either ridiculous or nonexistent.

While writing this book and bringing up these names my thoughts reflect back to Jerry who said, having Dave Barnes as my boss was a conflict of interest and he was going to have to retrain Dennis Gallagher and Al Galloway because they didn't recognize this situation as a conflict of interest. After looking at this list of names we hope retraining didn't just stop at those two. A final analysis of Dave Barnes being Vanguard's boss gave him the option to determine:

(1)   What area Vanguard could participate in
(2)   What jobs Vanguard could quote
(3)   That Dave Barnes could see vendors quotes and alter his to receive the purchase order.
(4)   That Dave Barnes had access to the database where increasing prices on his purchase orders could take place
(5)   That Triangle Commodity Group could eliminate Vanguard from competing against Barnes Tool.
(6)   And much more.

That's Delphi management at work.

When Vanguard Die and Machine took over the manufacturing and debugging of modules for Delphi there were hundreds of spare parts for the modules that Delphi no longer needed. During a conversation with Nicole, she suggested Vanguard buy these parts from Delphi. It wasn't too long after this conversation that Nicole informed Vanguard she was retiring and the final negotiation of these parts never took place. After Triangle Commodity Group took over the operation in the assembly die area a meeting was requested with Vanguard. Arnold Blunt, Cindy Silo, Bill Blasko, and I attended, with Cindy Silo, recording the minutes of the meeting. During the meeting Arnold Blunt reminded us there were hundreds of module **spare parts** in stock that Delphi no longer needed. Not long after the meeting we heard from Cindy silo notifying Vanguard the scrapping of obsolete parts was taking place and they were inquiring to see if Vanguard had any interest in going through a drum of scrap parts to see if there was anything we could use. A feeling came over us that Vanguard was being set up by Dave Barnes, so Vanguard declined the offer. If someone took the module spare parts they would be useless unless they were able to secure our blankets, and the only person that had that kind of control was our competitor Dave Barnes.

Luck came their way when Vanguard received a very large order for the modules. Cindy Silo from Triangle Commodity Group made a call to Vanguard acknowledging the large order for modules and they felt making an on time delivery would be difficult. She suggested, if delivery of these modules was going to be late to request a date change and they would accommodate us, and if we didn't they would work with us so Vanguard would not show a late delivery. Some of the orders Vanguard shipped to Delphi were late, but alterations of delivery dates never took place. What really took place was the hijacking of Vanguard Die and Machines modules by Dave Barnes. Vanguard received a call from Bill Blasko requesting a meeting to go over a few things.

A meeting was set to take place at Vanguard in approximately one week. Showing up for the meeting were Bill Blasko and Tony Bodine. As the meeting progressed with Triangle Commodity Group minor details were discussed, then the bombshell was dropped. Bill Blasko said that, since we were late on delivery of the modules Triangle Commodity Group was canceling the modules on our blankets and transferring the modules to Dave Barnes other company, Barnes Tool, and there was nothing Vanguard could do about it because they had the right to do whatever they wanted. As Bill Blasko and Tony Bodine were walking out of Vanguard's office you could hear them laughing.

A call was placed to Al Galloway and Dennis Gallagher and we explained the situation that took place between Dave Barnes and Vanguard. Al and Dennis stated, Dave Barnes can do whatever he wanted and that this situation does not sound like a conflict of interest.

After the transfer of the modules to Barnes Tool, Vanguard was curious about the on time delivery that Delphi's customers were receiving from Barnes Tool. A call was made to Arnold Blunt (his job was to inspect all modules before being sent to outside customers) and his response was that Barnes Tool was running between 2 to 4 weeks late on modules deliveries. According to Arnold, Delphi was receiving complaints from customers about the late deliveries and he also indicated that the majority of parts on the modules were stamped with old dates. Vanguard had no knowledge that these parts were at one time in Delphi's inventory, but you do wonder.

I came into contact with an executive from an automotive company and during our conversation I explained to him that Vanguard Die and Machine's fate was controlled by our competitor. At first there wasn't much interest, but as I explained how Dave Barnes's connection with Delphi's executives had cost Delphi's shareholders millions and millions of dollars his interest grew. The explanation of the control Dave Barnes had over Vanguard included what areas Vanguard could participate in, what jobs Vanguard could quote, how they could see our quotes and adjust their prices so they could award themselves the purchase orders, and how Dave Barnes had access to the database giving him the opportunity to raise prices on his orders if he chose, without competitive bidding. Dave Barnes could do anything he wanted according to Al Galloway and Dennis Gallagher.

The auto executive's first reaction was that I was joking. Since I was looking for a response, I asked him what would happen if this took place at his company under his watch. He could not give me an opinion about Delphi, but if this occurred at his company under his watch the following would happen.

(1)　This practice would be a conflict of interest, highly unethical and a major breach of trust.
(2)　At his company he would fire anyone that was involved in creating this scenario.
(3)　He would turn this over to and independent investigative agency to see if any criminal activity had occurred. If there was reason to believe there was criminal intent, they would prosecute

to the fullest extent of the law to ensure this would never happen again.

(4) Any person who knew about this and had the ability to issue contracts or recommend people or businesses to do work for his company would be reviewed. He would scrutinize those contracts to ensure honesty and integrity was foremost in management's agenda.

(5) If Triangle Commodity Group had contracts that were specifically awarded to cut costs and save his company money and Triangle Commodity Group intentionally prevented low cost suppliers from participating in the quoting process, his company would do everything possible to redeem their money.

I would imagine only 99.9% percent of the executives in this world would agree with him.

Having assemblies reassigned from Vanguard to Barnes Tool was not a one time deal. Vanguard had a die assembly on our blankets for years. After receiving a large order for these assemblies, a call from Cindy Silo was received inquiring whether Vanguard could make on time delivery. With the request of a thirty day delivery, Vanguard's estimate was about a fourty five day delivery. This was not acceptable to Triangle Commodity Group, so again they reassigned this purchase order to Barnes Tool. We were later informed that the delivery of the order arrived eight weeks late. Who scrutinized Dave Barnes's late deliveries? Oh yes, he reports to Dave Barnes. What a job!

It was obvious to Vanguard that our working relationship with Delphi, after almost twenty eight years was coming to an end. Vanguard figured another complaint to management was in order if only to get a reaction. It was Rick Cohan who Vanguard again contacted to inquire if there was someone at Delphi that had a little common sense. He instructed Vanguard to contact Dennis Gallagher to see if a connection with him could satisfy our concerns. When Vanguard had our initial contact with Dennis Gallagher our request was to see if he could direct Vanguard to the board of directors at Delphi with an e-mail address. The reason for requesting the e-mail address for the board of directors was to discuss the fact my competitor Dave Barnes was deciding the fate of Vanguard Die and Machine which in our eyes was clearly a conflict of interest.

Dennis's response was to have a three-way conversation on the phone that included Al Galloway. A time and day was set up for Vanguard to air our grievances.

At the beginning of the conversation, Al Galloway kept saying that Delphi had given Vanguard every opportunity to expand its presence at Delphi. After the third time we asked Al Galloway where this opportunity to grow was. No answer was forthcoming. It seemed that he was good at making claims but very poor at coming through with facts. As the conversation progressed, we pressed Al for some details as to where and when Vanguard's expansion was going to take place. Again Al developed lock jaw because all we heard was silence. Al Galloway and Dennis never responded to our initial request for the e-mail address of the Board of Directors at Delphi. We also brought up the fact Dave Barnes owned the company Triangle Commodity Group that decides Vanguard's fate at Delphi. He also owns the company Barnes Tool, where some of Vanguard's work was reassigned. Al Galloway and Dennis both felt this was not a conflict of interest. Vanguard brought to their attention that Dave Barnes had their ear and, any time Dave wanted, making up lies, twisting the truth, altering delivery dates, and more was all in their power.

We felt this was a major conflict of interest and just and just plain crazy. Al and Dennis stated that they thought Vanguard's dislike of Dave Barnes was clouding our judgment. We also brought to their attention that Triangle Commodity Group had control of the make die area in Warren, Ohio, whereVanguard had been one of the largest suppliers for approximately eighteen years. The explanation to Galloway and Dennis that Vanguard was sabotaged by Bill Blasko and Dean Hansen didn't seem to bother them. We inquired to see if they would or could help reinstate Vanguard in the make die area. Their response was that Vanguard had to check with Dave Barnes because he owned Triangle Commodity Group, which supervised that area. I am sure Dave Barnes was going to open up his arms to a major competitor for his other company Barnes Tool. The stupidity of these two Delphi employees in upper management was laughable.

When our complaints were heard by Jerry from Delphi's law Department, he stated that Galloway and Dennis were not acting in the best interest of Delphi, because this was definitely a conflict of interest and even though Galloway and Dennis were Delphi employees the retraining of these two employees was a priority in the near future. Without strong guidance and common sense from management this is what you get: stupidity, the loss of millions of dollars, and bankruptcy.

During the conversation with Al and Dennis it was brought to our attention that Vanguard had been put on hold by our competitors Triangle Commodity Group because of late deliveries. I'm sure Triangle Commodity Group informed Galloway and Dennis when Barnes Tool was two months late on die assemblies and four weeks late on modules. Besides that they can alter their late delivery dates. Where's the common sense at Delphi management? Vanguard didn't expect to receive much assistance from Galloway or Dennis,, but their reaction to our complaints was important to us. Having a conversation with two stupid idiots at Delphi management made the direction Vanguard took next, a lot easier.

When Triangle Commodity Group reassigned the modules Vanguard had on blankets, this left us with hundreds of extra spare parts. Thinking we would receive the same reaction from Triangle Commodity Group that we receive from John when we requested Delphi Mexico to buy the extra parts we had in stock after our blankets were not renewed.

These spare parts are still active today, but the response we received from John in Mexico was silence.

Vanguard took it upon ourselves to dispose of these extra assembly die spare parts in our own way, in doing so we were hoping to get a response from Delphi's legal Department. Knowing Vanguard's opportunity at Delphi was closing fast, we decided to sell the extra spare parts on the open market. In the early part of 2012 Vanguard took out an advertisement in a wiring harness magazine. Since the modules and assemblies were for outside sales, there was a market for the extra dies, spare parts, and modules that Vanguard had in stock. This must have triggered Delphi's legal department into action because Vanguard did receive a response from their legal Department asking Vanguard to refrain from selling the modules and spare parts in the open market. Vanguard's response to the legal Department was to describe our grievances with Delphi's management and how over the years Delphi lost millions and millions of dollars through:

(1)   The sabotaging of Vanguard by Bill Blasko and Dean Hansen in the make die area.
(2)   Dale Beck allowed Dave Barnes to overcharge Delphi millions and millions of dollars.
(3)   Dave Barnes was awarded the Mexico assemblies without going through the bidding process.
(4)   Dave Barnes became Vanguard Die and Machines boss.
(5)   The removal of assemblies by Triangle Commodity Group Commodity group from Vanguard's blankets and reassigning them to Barnes Tool, both owned by our competitor Dave Barnes and much more.

We also indicated that with the help of Sam Haack, Nicole Smith, Dick Winner, and Jack Hagan the loyal Delphi employees, some of these affronts were overturned, saving Delphi millions of dollars.

Not only did the legal Department request Vanguard not to sell the modules and spare parts on the open market, but they were concerned about our grievances towards Delphi management. A breath of fresh air was taken in when Jerry an investigator for Delphi's legal Department requested a meeting with Vanguard. Within a week Vanguard met with

Jerry, so he could get a better understanding of what had taken place in the past.

We were a little disappointed with Jerry's agenda. His main concern was when and how Dave Barnes of Triangle Commodity Group received the position of overseeing his competitors, giving him the opportunity to regulate his competition. We explained to Jerry, Vanguard has no firsthand knowledge of how this situation took place and that, we can only relay the information we heard. George Sorry went out for quotes, then approached Dave Barnes with an offer to take control of the make die area. After George and Dave reached an agreement, Jack Hagan was instructed to push the agreement through purchasing.

We discussed the other incidents that affected Vanguard and cost Delphi millions upon millions of dollars. Jerry was looking for a way to verify our statements. His focus seemed to center around the employees still at Delphi, as he was in the position to question them. His last request was whether we could furnish any e-mails or documents that could help his case. After Delphi's management started sabotaging Vanguard and bypassing our blankets to favor their friends, we started saving e-mails and correspondence with Delphi management. We put together a group of e-mails and correspondence that Jerry requested that substantiated our position. The next day we met with Jerry to complete our transfer of the e-mails and correspondence.

It took Jerry approximately three weeks to get back to Vanguard with his report. With the information that we furnished to Jerry our thought was that an in-depth investigation would be carried out. That didn't happen, the only thing Jerry wanted to focus on was whether or not the access that Dave Barnes had to our quotes, blankets, and our future at Delphi was a conflict of interest. The access to these items that Dave Barnes had, did much more than simply allow large sums of money to change hands; it also affected the lives of our employees. Due to the ineffective management at Delphi, many employees at Vanguard lost their jobs. I wonder how Bill Blasko, Dean Hansen, Dale Beck, and many others in management would feel if they lost their jobs. Jerry's report indicated a conflict of interest had been taking place over the past seven years. The majority of Vanguard's employees were lost over that period of time. So in 2013 Vanguard Die and Machine close their doors and was put up for sale.